Don Quixote de la Mancha

Juan de la Cuesta Hispanic Monographs

SERIES: UCLA Center for 17th- and 18th-Century Studies:
The *Comedia* in Translation and Performance, Nº 17

FOUNDING EDITOR
Tom Lathrop †
University of Delaware

PUBLISHER
Michael P. Bolan
University of Delaware

EDITOR
Michael J. McGrath
Georgia Southern University

EDITORIAL BOARD
Vincent Barletta
Stanford University

Annette Grant Cash
Georgia State University

David Castillo
State University of New York-Buffalo

Gwen Kirkpatrick
Georgetown University

Mark P. Del Mastro
College of Charleston

Juan F. Egea
University of Wisconsin-Madison

Sara L. Lehman
Fordham University

Mariselle Meléndez
University of Illinois at Urbana-Champaign

Eyda Merediz
University of Maryland

Dayle Seidenspinner-Núñez
University of Notre Dame

Elzbieta Sklodowska
Washington University in St. Louis

Noël Valis
Yale University

Guillén de Castro

Don Quixote de la Mancha

Translated by

The UCLA Working Group
on the *Comedia* in Translation and Performance:

Barbara Fuchs
Rafael Jaime
Brenda Saraí Jaramillo
Rachel Kaufman
Robin Kello
Javier Patiño Loira
Aina Soley Mateu
Dandi Meng

Laura Muñoz
Marta Albalá Pelegrín
Victoria Rasbridge
Amanda Riggle
Rhonda Sharrah
Sammy Solis
Jesslyn Whittell

Juan de la Cuesta
Newark, Delaware

Our translations are free to use for educational and performance purposes with attribution to Diversifying the Classics, under a Creative Commons Attribution 4.0 International License. We are happy to discuss and consult on performances and adaptations. Notify us at diversifyingtheclassics.ucla@gmail.com prior to use.

Copyright © 2025 by Barbara Fuchs. All rights reserved.

Juan de la Cuesta Hispanic Monographs
An imprint of LinguaText, LLC
103 Walker Way
Newark, Delaware 19711 USA
(302) 453-8695

www.JuandelaCuesta.com

Manufactured in the United States of America
ISBN: 978-1-58871-409-1

Table of Contents

The *Comedia* in Context 7
A Note on the Playwright 11

Introduction
    Laura Muñoz and Jesslyn Whittell 13
Pronunciation Guide 27

Don Quixote de la Mancha
    Characters 28
    Act I 29
    Act II 64
    Act III 114

The *Comedia* in Context

THE "GOLDEN AGE" OF Spain offers one of the most vibrant theatrical repertoires ever produced. At the same time that England saw the flourishing of Shakespeare on the Elizabethan stage, Spain produced prodigious talents such as Lope de Vega, Tirso de Molina, and Calderón de la Barca. Although those names may not resonate with the force of the Bard in the Anglophone world, the hundreds of entertaining, complex plays they wrote, and the stage tradition they helped develop, deserve to be better known.

The *Diversifying the Classics* project at UCLA brings these plays to the public by offering English versions of Hispanic classical theater. Our translations are designed to make this rich tradition accessible to students, teachers, and theater professionals. This brief introduction to the *comedia* in its context suggests what we might discover and create when we begin to look beyond Shakespeare.

COMEDIA AT A GLANCE

The Spanish *comedia* developed in the late sixteenth and early seventeenth centuries. As Madrid grew into a sophisticated imperial capital, the theater provided a space to perform the customs, concerns, desires, and anxieties of its citizens. Though the form was influenced by the Italian troupes that brought *commedia dell'arte* to Spain in the sixteenth century, the expansive corpus of the Spanish *comedia* includes not only comic plays, but also histories, tragedies, and tragicomedies. The varied dramatic template of the *comedia* is as diverse as the contemporary social sphere it reflects.

While the plays offer a range of dramatic scenarios and theatrical effects, they share structural and linguistic similarities. Roughly three thousand lines, they are usually divided into three different *jornadas*, or acts. Plots move quickly across time and space, without much regard for the Aristotelian unities of action, time, and place. The plays are written in verse, and employ different forms for different characters and situations: a lover may deliver an ornate sonnet in honor of the beloved, while a servant offers a shaggy-dog story in rhymed couplets. The plays' language is designed for the ear rather than the eye, with the objective of pleasing an audience.

The *comedia* was performed in rectangular courtyard spaces known as *corrales*. Built between houses of two or three stories, the *corral* offered seating based on social position, including space for the nobles in the balconies, women in the *cazuela*, or stewpot, and *mosqueteros*, or groundlings, on patio benches. This cross-section of society enjoyed a truly popular art, which reflected onstage their varied social positions. A *comedia* performance would have included the play as well as songs, dances, and *entremeses*, or short comic interludes, before, after, and between the acts. As the first real commercial theater, the corral was the place where a diverse urban society found its dramatic entertainment.

What's at Stake on the *Comedia* Stage?

Comedias offer a range of possibilities for the twenty-first century reader, actor, and audience. The plays often envision the social ambitions and conflicts of the rapidly-growing cities where they were performed, allowing a community to simultaneously witness and create a collective culture. In many *comedias*, the anonymity and wealth that the city affords allow the clever to transcend their social position, while wit, rather than force, frequently carries the day, creating an urban theater that itself performs urbanity. An important subset of *comedias* deal with topics from national history, exploring violence, state power, the role of the nobility, and religious and racial difference.

The *comedia* often examines social hierarchies that may be less rigid than they first appear. Whether the dominant mode of the play is comic, tragic, historical, or a mixture, its dramatic progression often depends on a balancing act of order and liberty, authority and transgression, stasis and transformation. The title of Lope de Vega's recently rediscovered *Women and Servants*, in which two sisters scheme to marry the servant-men they love rather than the noblemen who woo them, makes explicit its concerns with gender and class and provides a view of what is at stake in many of the plays. Individuals disadvantaged by class or gender often challenge the social hierarchy and patriarchy by way of their own cleverness. The *gracioso* (comic sidekick), the *barba* (older male blocking figure), and the lovers appear repeatedly in these plays, and yet are often much more than stock types. At their most remarkable, they reflect larger cultural possibilities. The *comedia* stages the conflicting demands of desire and reputation, dramatizing the tension between our identities as they are and as we wish them to be.

Among the many forms of passion and aspiration present in the *comedia*, female desire and agency are central. In contrast to its English counterpart, the Spanish stage permitted actresses to play female roles, thus giving playwrights the opportunity to develop a variety of characters for them. While actresses became famous, the powerful roles they played onstage often portrayed the force of female desire. In Lope's *The Widow of Valencia*, for example, the beautiful young widow Leonarda brings a masked lover into her home so as not to reveal her identity and risk her reputation or independence.

The presence of actresses, however, did not diminish the appeal of the cross-dressing plot. One of Tirso's most famous plays, *Don Gil of the Green Breeches*, features Doña Juana assuming a false identity and dressing as a man in order to foil the plans of her former lover, who is also in disguise. Dizzying deceptions and the performance of identity are both dramatic techniques and thematic concerns in these plays. Gender, like class, becomes part of the structure the *comedia* examines and dismantles, offering a powerful reflection on how we come to be who we are.

Remaking Plays in Our Time

In Lope's witty manifesto, the *New Art of Making Plays in Our Time*, he advises playwrights to stick to what works onstage, including plots of honor and love, strong subplots, and—whenever possible—cross-dressing. For Lope, the delight of the audience drives the process of composition, and there is little sense in a craft that does not entertain the public. Lope's contemporaries followed this formula, developing dramas that simultaneously explore the dynamics of their society and produce spectacle. For this reason, early modern Hispanic drama remains an engaging, suspenseful, often comic—and new—art to audiences even four hundred years later.

The *Diversifying the Classics* project at UCLA, engaged in translation, adaptation, and outreach to promote the *comedia* tradition, aims to bring the entertaining spirit of Lope and his contemporaries to our work. Rather than strictly adhering to the verse forms of the plays, we seek to render the power of their language in a modern idiom; rather than limiting the drama as a historical or cultural artifact, we hope to bring out what remains vibrant for our contemporary society. Given that these vital texts merit a place onstage, we have sought to facilitate production by carefully noting entrances, exits, and asides, and by adding locations for scenes whenever possible. Although we have translated every line, we assume directors will cut as appropriate for their own productions. We hope that actors, directors, and readers will translate our work further into new productions, bringing both the social inquiry and theatrical delight of the *comedia* to future generations of audiences.

A Note on the Playwright

GUILLÉN DE CASTRO Y BELVIS (1569–1631) was a Valencian playwright whose theatrical oeuvre developed along with the genre of *comedia* itself. Like many of his contemporaries, he was a military man as well as a poet: in addition to serving as a captain of the guard for Valencia's coast in 1593, he also briefly served as governor of a district of Naples. Not much is known about his time in Italy, although it is evident that he continued to write plays during this time. After retiring from military duties, Castro decided to try his luck as a playwright in the capital city of Madrid, publishing a collection of his plays with the last of his money in 1619 and pinning all his hopes on selling those volumes to get him out of debt. One of the plays in this collection was his adaptation of *Don Quixote de la Mancha*.

Although only twenty-six of his plays were published in his lifetime (by Castro himself), most scholars agree that he wrote a total of thirty-five. His plays vary from the mythological to the urban, yet all show the influences of a Valencian tradition as well as dramatic techniques, themes, and characters that are unique to his oeuvre. Castro was not afraid to tackle subjects which were considered highly taboo in Spanish society and on the stage, in particular regicide, bigamy, and sexuality. Castro's works address the factors that shape identity, including gender; power and authority, especially as exercised by rulers over their subjects; and the troubled domestic relationships of husbands and wives. His plays often portray the dramatic lives of the nobility, adapting legendary figures from Iberian history and ballads to the stage, as in his best-known play, *Las mocedades del Cid*, which became the basis for Pierre Corneille's *Le Cid*. He was fully engaged with his contemporaries across literary genres, and his skill in translating popular stories, like the ballads of the Cid or Don Quixote's exploits, as well as his unflinching presentation of urban life, make him one of the most interesting playwrights of Spanish *comedia*.

Introduction
Laura Muñoz and Jesslyn Whittell

Guillén de Castro's *Don Quixote de la Mancha* brings together iconic characters from Miguel de Cervantes's masterpiece in an adaptation based on the captivating Cardenio subplot that also inspired Shakespeare's lost play. This version is reimagined for the stage with a plot about infants switched at birth, the demands and limitations of nobility, and the obstacles characters must overcome to find justice and happiness. The titular Don Quixote and his trusty squire Sancho Panza find themselves tangled in stories of love and desire, providing comic relief as they make their way through the plot, forever lost in chivalrous fantasies.

The Plot
The action opens *in medias res* as the noble **Lucinda** almost falls with her horse down a precipice and **Cardenio**, her beloved and a servant of the **Duke**, comes to her rescue. After six years of secret courtship, Lucinda is so determined to discover why Cardenio hasn't proposed marriage that she has followed the Duke's hunting party to speak to her beloved. Yet their conversation is quickly interrupted by the **Marqués,** son of the Duke, in hot pursuit of **Dorotea**, a shepherdess. Dorotea is saved from the Marqués's advances by a bear attack on the Duke's hunting party offstage. While the Marqués pretends not to hear and runs away, Cardenio hastens to help the Duke. Cardenio makes quick work of the threat and the two return to the clearing, where Lucinda hides in order not to be seen. The Duke praises Cardenio and curses his son as a coward, stating, not for the last time, that he wishes Cardenio were his son instead. The Duke and Cardenio make their way to the Duke's tent for first aid, and Lucinda remains hidden long enough to witness the Marqués once again attempting to seduce Dorotea. While Dorotea insists that a union between them would come to no good end because she is a peasant and he a nobleman, the Marqués wears down her resolve by promising

to marry her. She asks for time to think about it, then hides in the bushes when the Duke appears with the peasant **Lisardo**. With this arrival, Lucinda discovers that Cardenio is the son of a peasant. Once they are able to speak again, Cardenio confesses his lie of omission, offering his dagger to Lucinda as a sign that he's at her mercy, but she declares that she still loves him. When Dorotea and the Marqués are alone again, she rejects him and threatens to start yelling unless he lets her go. **Don Quixote** then makes his appearance, shouting for **Sancho** to hurry so they can save the damsel in distress.

Quixote announces himself as a knight errant who defends the defenseless, but the Marqués, angry at the interruption, directs his servants to attack Quixote. Dorotea escapes in the chaos, followed by the Marqués. Quixote, injured and on the ground, tries to explain to Sancho that he needs a confessor because he's on his deathbed when the **Priest** and the **Barber**, friends of the would-be knight, appear. The Priest doesn't have much chance to chastise Quixote before the Duke appears again with his servants, who warn him that Quixote is a crazy man. Quixote introduces himself and while the Priest and Duke play along with him, the Barber explains to the Duke who Quixote is and why he is wandering in the woods. Meanwhile, Quixote confesses his sins, to which the Priest replies that his penance is to return home. The first act ends with the Duke's offer to see to Quixote's wounds while Quixote shouts about how he's dying.

The Marqués appears at the top of Act II, scheming about how to release himself from Dorotea after having successfully seduced her. When Cardenio walks in, the Marqués asks him for advice. Yet he soon finds his own solution: Cardenio must marry Dorotea, leaving the Marqués free to pursue Lucinda. Cardenio immediately refuses this offer, explaining that although he sees the Marqués as a brother, having been raised in the same household by Lisardo when they were younger, and although he is himself a peasant, he too is honorable, and does not want to marry the woman the Marqués is trying to get rid of. Lucinda appears, making it clear that the Marqués is courting her and also that she prefers Cardenio. She pretends to trip and slips Cardenio a letter as he helps her up. The Marqués escorts her away, leaving Cardenio behind to read the note where Lucinda tells him that her father has decided that she will marry the Marqués. Cardenio can't contain himself and, when the Marqués returns, he begs him to pursue a different woman. The Marqués, angry that a peasant would aspire to such a beauty, promises to help Cardenio while plotting to ruin him.

The next scene opens with Dorotea crying next to a fountain over her misfortune, as Don Quixote and Sancho come upon her. Sancho challenges

Quixote's poetic description of their surroundings as a fantastical castle and Dorotea as a weeping princess, recognizing her as the cause of Quixote's earlier injuries. Lucinda appears, telling Dorotea and her father **Fideno** that she needs to recover with them until she feels better, while her father rides on to one of their country estates. Dorotea begins to ask Lucinda what's wrong, only to be interrupted by Quixote barreling into their conversation with offers to help. Lucinda, annoyed, comes up with a nonsense task for Quixote to get rid of him: he must escort Lucinda's servants on the road. He sets off happily, without knowing where they are or how to get there.

Once the two women are alone, Lucinda confides her woes to Dorotea: her father is making her marry a man she doesn't love instead of her true love. Just then the Marqués arrives with Lucinda's servant. Dorotea is shocked, as she believes the Marqués is the true love Lucinda spoke of. Lucinda, however, has arranged to meet the Marqués to confess her love for Cardenio and ask his help in preventing the wrong marriage. The Marqués pretends to agree so that she will leave with him. Lucinda gets back in her carriage, but Dorotea manages to stop the Marqués from leaving, demanding that he answer for what has occurred between them. He escapes her without answering, leaving Dorotea to curse her former love to hell.

As she tries to exit, Quixote re-enters with Lucinda's servants. Distractable as he is, Quixote tries to follow Dorotea, but Lucinda's servants scold him for trying to abandon his "duty" as their escort. Quixote agrees to focus on the task at hand and has a flirtatious exchange with Lucinda's ladies-in-waiting, though the teasing ends when Sancho appears to tell Quixote that there's trouble with his horse Rocinante and Quixote runs off to deal with it.

In the next scene, Lucinda has been locked up by her father until she agrees to marry the Marqués. When Dorotea comes by, disguised as a young man in order to track down the Marqués, Lucinda pleads with her to bring a message to Cardenio about where she is and what's going on. It is now nighttime and Quixote has arrived at the same house where Lucinda has been locked up. Quixote, believing he is the mythological Leander, confuses Lucinda's light in the window (a signal for Cardenio) as a signal for him. He has Sancho help him undress so that he can swim across the imaginary seas to reach his imagined lover. Cardenio and Dorotea arrive at the house too late to help Lucinda, but in time to have the **Matron** slip them into the wedding.

Inside, Lucinda's father **Teodoro** hands her off to the Marqués so they can be married, with Dorotea and Cardenio spying at the doors. Everyone waits in suspense to see what Lucinda will say, and when she says yes, Cardenio runs off without seeing how the wedding plays out. Dorotea, however, witnesses how Lucinda faints and is then found to be carrying a dagger and a suicide note. The Marqués vows to make her life miserable, bringing the second act to a close.

Act III opens with **Fulgencio**, the Duke's servant, recapping the events of the ill-fated wedding. Neither the Marqués nor Cardenio has been seen since. This shocking news leads the Duke to confess to Fulgencio his doubts about the Marqués's parentage, explaining that his son was born out of wedlock and given to the peasant Lisardo to raise until the Duke's father died and he was finally able to bring his wife and son home. The Marqués has always been so awful that the Duke has harbored doubts about whether Lisardo returned the right boy to him. This conversation is interrupted by Teodoro, who seeks an audience to ask the Duke's help in finding Lucinda, also missing since the wedding. Next Fideno arrives, seeking the Duke's help in restoring Dorotea's honor, to which the Duke replies that the Marqués will pay with his life for the dishonor done to Dorotea. Finally, Lucinda comes in for an audience, explaining how she escaped after the botched wedding and asking for the Duke's protection, a request he agrees to as well.

In the next scene, Quixote and Sancho appear, having found a sack containing a sword, cape, and hat, which Sancho is very excited about. The two come across a peasant, and, much to Sancho's dismay, Quixote asks if he knows who the sack belong to. The peasant tells them that the sack belongs to a madman who has been rampaging in the countryside, surviving by stealing food from laborers like himself. Cardenio himself appears then in nothing but underclothes, waxing poetic about lost loves and betrayal. When Quixote tries to talk to him, Cardenio responds by attacking the three men, leaving Quixote very inspired by this display of madness. He gives Sancho a letter to deliver to his imagined lover Dulcinea, explaining that he'll be smashing his head against rocks for a while to show how much he loves her.

Next the Priest and Barber make their return, this time speaking with a lucid Cardenio, who recounts his bout of madness to them. Sancho appears, on his way to deliver the letter, and is stopped by the Barber and Priest. After Sancho explains his errand, the men begin brainstorming about how to get their friend home, only to hear a voice nearby. The men follow the sound of the voice and find Dorotea, disguised as a boy, who provides Cardenio with the missing context about Lucinda's attempted suicide, as well as her letter. The two decide to return to the Duke's palace to chase down their respective loves, but the Priest asks if they'll first help get Quixote off the mountain and back home, which they agree to do.

In the meantime, Quixote has once again stripped down in imitation of Cardenio (as well as the chivalric heroes of his books). Sancho escorts Dorotea, now posing as a "Princess Micomicona", to the clearing. She recounts a fanciful story about losing her kingdom, which Quixote immediately believes, and he decides to help her. Back at the Duke's palace, all the conflicts come to a head as Cardenio challenges the Marqués, but before they can fight, Lisardo bursts in to declare that his wife has just died. He explains that on her deathbed she confessed to switching the two babies at birth, which means that Cardenio is actually the Duke's son and the Marqués is really the peasants' son. The Duke shouts that he knew it all along, and Cardenio immediately takes Lucinda's hand in marriage, commanding that the ex-Marqués take Dorotea as his wife, which he meekly agrees to. As the couples pair off, the Barber and Priest re-appear onstage with Quixote in a cage, ready to take him back home. Quixote isn't too bothered by this once they tell him a prophecy about his adventure not being over, and thus ends the play.

Adapting The Novel

Don Quixote de la Mancha could rightly be called the most famous Spanish novel of all time, as well as the first modern novel. Written by Miguel de Cervantes and published in two parts (1605, 1615), the novel follows the adventures of a minor Spanish nobleman in Castile who reads so many chivalric romances that he loses his mind and decides to go out and be a knight, attempting to right wrongs in the world under the name of Don Quixote. The core of the novel lies in its constant interplay between truth, deception, reality, and illusion, all delivered with a sense of irony and ingenuity that continues to engage readers. When first published, the novel about the delusional man who believed himself a knight in shining armor was an instant success. Almost immediately, the novel's iconic characters took on a life of their own in popular culture, where they have continued to thrive ever since.

There are no clear dates for when Guillén de Castro wrote his *Don Quijote*, though most scholars believe it was written between 1605 and 1610, and certainly published by 1618. In this adaptation, Castro stages what is known as the Cardenio episode, a story which unfolds from Chapter 23 through Chapter 37 of Part I of Cervantes's novel. The episode begins when Quixote and Sancho spot a wild man in the Sierra Morena. He is actually an Andalusian noble named Cardenio, who tells a sorry tale about being driven mad with grief over his betrayal by Lucinda, the woman he loves, and Fernando, a duke's son whom he serves. Over the course of thirteen chapters, the narrative reveals the interrelated stories of Cardenio and Dorotea, a well-off but low-born woman who was seduced and abandoned by Fernando, told from a variety of perspectives, until in Chapter 36 Fernando and Lucinda themselves appear to tell their own stories and resolve matters between them. While the Cardenio episode becomes the driving narrative force of much of Part I, there is no doubt that they are still featured guests in Quixote's story.

Castro's adaptation creates a streamlined narrative from the very fractured storytelling found in the original. The play takes the meandering and oft-interrupted plot of the novel and restructures the narrative into a three-act *comedia* by establishing new character relationships in the first act, and, most importantly, by shifting the focus away from Quixote and Sancho. Rather than the stories of Cardenio and Dorotea being retold as past events in and around Quixote's adventures, these characters take center stage while the would-be knight and his squire become the comic relief. Castro's Act II introduces many recognizable plot points from the novel: Quixote and Sancho find Cardenio's belongings in the wilderness before meeting Cardenio and hearing part of his tale; Quixote, inspired by Cardenio, decides to strip naked until his lady Dulcinea grants him a response to a love letter which Sancho never delivers; the Priest and Barber, looking for Quixote, find the disguised Dorotea and ask for her help impersonating a princess. The play even ends with the knight errant locked in a cage, ready to be transported back to La Mancha as in the ending of the 1605 novel.

Although condensing this diffuse plot is integral to recreating the Cardenio story for theater, Castro does allude to the original fragmented storytelling in the staging of the play, especially in scenes where a character, or characters, secretly spy on the action occurring onstage. This happens especially throughout the first act, with Dorotea and Lucinda often bearing witness to private moments, although at no point do any of the characters have all the information. The reveal that Cardenio and the Marqués were switched as infants is only surprising to the characters, as the audience knows about the Duke's misgivings from Act I. Indeed, the switched-at-birth plot, a fabrication added by Castro, simplifies some of the more complex elements of the novel, making Cardenio's supposed peasant status what prevents his marriage to Lucinda, as opposed to the various pressures that impede the union in the novel. Dorotea's story is also softened in this retelling, as Castro restages the relationship to encompass both the possibility of sexual coercion by the Marqués and an ongoing, if aggressive, flirtation between the characters where Dorotea nevertheless holds her own. Perhaps the biggest departure in this regard is that the play has no equivalent scene to the one in the novel where Fernando enters Dorotea's bedroom without permission in order to complete his "seduction." In the play, sexual violence remains implicit in all their interactions, yet Dorotea's agency remains at the forefront. Taken together, these changes create a cohesive theatrical work which shifts the focus while remaining a *Quixote*-inspired tale.

The Comedic Stylings of Quixote and Sancho

When Don Quixote first appears in this play, the stage directions tell us that he enters "*astride Rocinante, dressed just as described in the book*" (Act I, Scene 1). In the novel, Quixote is described as tall and thin, with a weathered face, deep-set eyes, and a long, silver beard. His attire reflects his delusional mindset, as he adorns himself in a mishmash of outdated armor and a battered helmet that is eventually replaced by the iconic barber's basin. While Quixote's appearance is striking, his defining characteristics are his vivid imagination, his relentless desire to bring about justice and protect the weak, and his propensity for getting into trouble. There are countless instances in the novel of the wannabe knight getting the business end of a club to the face, reprised in several instances of slapstick violence in the play.

Quixote's commitment to chivalric ideals in a decidedly un-chivalric 17th century is what propels him into this play, as Dorotea's cries while trying to get away from the Marqués draw him to the scene. Immediately taken down by the Marqués's servants, Quixote begins to refer to himself as Valdovinos, entering one of the many sustained delusions that reference earlier literary works that still circulated, both orally and in print, in Quixote's time. In this case it is the *Ballad of the Marqués of Mantua*, a 15th-century poem that describes the knight Valdovinos being grievously wounded by a rival in love, only to be found near death by his uncle, the Marqués of Mantua. Quixote plays his part perfectly, and luckily for him the stories he references are well-known enough that the Duke and Priest can play along at the end of Act I.

A major component of Cervantes's novel is exactly the kind of imitation of chivalric figures that features in this scene and many others: Quixote imitates famous characters, plucking from an endless supply of references whatever suits the situation at hand. In this play, he takes on the role of the tragic lover from the Greek myth of Hero and Leander, as well as the mad Orlando from Italian Renaissance epic and the lovelorn Amadís from Spanish chivalric novels. Quixote's delusions are varied in origin but have many elements in common, including tragic ends and failing (at least temporarily) in love. Much of the humor in the play comes from Quixote's embodiment of these characters, all examples of over-the-top emotionality juxtaposed with the very low stakes of Quixote's own reality. These jokes serve a double function, as their metatheatricality makes us reflect on all the different roles we play when in love.

Quixote's famous sidekick Sancho Panza helps to underscore this juxtaposition, as his role is to entertain the delusions of his master while never really getting caught up in them. Sancho's character reflects a far more pragmatic outlook on life, concerned with practical matters. For example, when the two encounter a mad Cardenio, Sancho is far less concerned with the lover's tragic tale than with the issue of whether or not he'll get to keep the man's clothing. This contrast between his practicality and Don Quixote's idealism leads to frequent clashes and humorous exchanges between the two characters, with Sancho providing a grounded perspective on the world and comically noting the absurdity of Quixote's actions. Such is the case in Act II, when they come across Dorotea's home:

> DON QUIXOTE   We've arrived at a castle.
> SANCHO   A house, you mean. (lines 1193-4)

Sancho's role throughout the play is to provide commentary, as well as not-quite-sarcastic responses to Quixote's impassioned proclamations on love, honor, and chivalry. Sancho is also known for his humorous and colloquial speech patterns: he speaks in proverbs and sayings, often creating confusion or providing amusing insights as part of his color commentary.

The most surprising thing about Quixote and Sancho in this adaptation is how little we actually see of them. The two mostly play the role of periodic comic relief, yet Castro still chose to title his play *Don Quixote*. Perhaps this is because the figure was so popular, then as now, or perhaps because they make a splash whenever they arrive on stage. While it's true that the play's story comes to us more or less intact from Cervantes's novel, the knight and his squire are shifted to the periphery. Nevertheless, their comedic moments counterbalance the more serious tone of the lovers' travails and are sure to steal the show.

Finding the Comedy in *Comedia*

One of the most exciting—and simultaneously jarring—aspects of this play is the relationship between comedy and the more serious strains of the plot. Cardenio and Lucinda's relationship is the driving force of the play, with the action rising toward Lucinda's forced marriage to and kidnapping at the hands of the Marqués and her near suicide. Yet, while the other characters struggle with issues of class, power, and love, Don Quixote and Sancho rove through a fanciful world peopled with knights and ladies. (Ironically, those books of chivalry include their own versions of marriage plots, which are often resolved through magic, the supernatural, or, in a powerful link with this play, through the miraculous discovery of noble origins.) At times, the play seems to be telling two stories, so much so that by the end Quixote's function is almost a distraction: he impedes the resolution of the marriage plot by forcing Dorotea and Cardenio to put their own troubles on pause while they try to get him home.

While this rapid-fire transition between serious matter and comedy was in fact common for Hispanic Golden Age drama—as for English plays like *Arden of Faversham* or *The Knight of the Burning Pestle* (itself based on *Don Quixote*) and some of Shakespeare's own tragicomedies, like *A Winter's Tale*—it rattles the genre conventions that modern audiences are accustomed to. Yet the tension between the comedy and romance in this play is its motor: the real delight is in watching how these unlikely stories weave together. As the drama mounts, Lucinda finds herself forced into marriage with the Marqués and threatens to kill herself. This entire sequence echoes a bizarre interlude with Don Quixote in the previous scene, where, in an ill-fated attempt to flirt with a young Maid, he determines that she must be "Hero" and he must be "Leander". Quixote is alluding to the Greek myth, where Leander and Hero court for a summer before parting for the winter. One night, the lovelorn Leander sees the light Hero keeps in her tower and decides to swim to her across the rough waters that divide them. He follows the guidance of Hero's light until the wind blows it out, after which he gets lost and drowns. Tragic as the myth is, the scene with Quixote is pure slapstick—the stage directions seem to suggest that the actor strips on stage and mimes swimming across the floor.

This improbable, almost embarrassing, sequence with Quixote sets the stage for the scene with Lucinda, as several of the same images, concepts, and circumstances are recycled. Cardenio, like Quixote's character Leander, is separated from his love and looking for a light in the tower. The play seems to suggest that comedy and romance are not terribly different: even if they appear ridiculous, the fantastical stories of Quixote's world end up providing the narrative elements for the story of Cardenio and Lucinda. In other words, here and elsewhere in the play, Quixote's storyline often anticipates and even seems to precipitate the developments of the "real life" plot, which allows the play to comment on how tropes recycle themselves across genres and periods. The play literalizes the idea that the stories we tell ourselves shape our lived realities.

As with Cervantes's novel, the push and pull between these two tones is a deliberate commentary on the shifting nature of storytelling and the narratives we use to make sense of our experiences. Quixote inhabits a fading kind of narrative, and a fading way of thinking, while the characters he meets struggle with the challenges of early modernity. Yet, in both the novel and the play, Quixote doesn't always come out the worse for wear. His idealized vision of the world, while undeniably ridiculous, satirizes the cruelty and unpredictability of the characters around him. However silly Quixote's chivalry looks in the play, the violent world of the marriage plots, where characters like Dorotea, Cardenio, and Lucinda are caught up in the demands of class structures and money, often comes out looking much worse.

These similarities are a key site for interpretation and experimentation by productions. We recommend playing up the contrast between the different plots for comedic effect, but casting, set, sound, or prop choices might be used to highlight the similarities between Quixote's storyline and those of the marriage plots.

Nobility and Social Class

A central question for this play is the nature of nobility—whether it is an inherent trait of the upper class or the result of their privilege and wealth. It's a question we're encouraged to attend to from the first few scenes. In Act I, the Marqués, who as the Duke's son has considerable wealth and status, nevertheless shows himself to be both a predator and a coward: he pursues Dorotea against her will, yet runs off when his father's hunting party is attacked by a bear. Meanwhile Cardenio is respectful and devoted in his courtship of Lucinda, and rushes to help the Duke when he hears his call. The irony here, one that would be very apparent to a 17th-century audience, is that the supposed nobleman shows none of the courage or chivalry that a man in his position "should" have, while the peasant's son displays all of these virtues. In fact, the play goes to great lengths to establish Cardenio and the Marqués as foils. As we later learn, both men were raised together by Cardenio's father, the peasant Lisardo. To really drive the point home, the Duke laments that he wishes Cardenio were his son instead.

Act I thus challenges traditional assumptions about nobility. Status is no guarantor of virtue and, as the Marqués's behavior with Dorotea indicates, is more often used to manipulate and abuse others than to protect them. Even Lucinda, after learning that Cardenio is a peasant's son and that the nature of his birth has prevented him from proposing to her, nevertheless decides "Though you are born of these fields, / you shall be mine / and I shall be yours" (lines 547-9). Yet by Act III, we see the play taking a different angle. The Duke returns to his earlier theme, but this time voices his hunch that Cardenio is in fact his biological son, switched with the Marqués by Lisardo and his wife. He makes this inference based on the behavior of each man: Cardenio acts like a nobleman, therefore he must be one, and vice versa. This assumption turns out to be dead on, and once the nature of Cardenio's parentage comes to light, the story's romantic tensions resolve. To some extent, this ending undoes the play's previous challenges to nobility. The message we're left with seems to be that nobility is so powerful, so profoundly inherent, that it will surface in a person's actions even when their heritage is unknown. While this conclusion might be disappointing, it is hardly surprising. At the same time, the play introduces several complications to its own conclusion and makes several key alterations to the original Cervantes plot.

The first major complication is Dorotea, who from Act I indicates that she not only accepts but prefers her life as a shepherdess, particularly in contrast to the coldness and formality of courtly life. "Though my position is low, / I prize it as my own" (lines 606-7). What Dorotea values about her world is the freedom it affords her, a freedom unavailable to Lucinda, as we see in Act II. Indeed, Lucinda is at the mercy of her father for most of the play, while Dorotea, dressed as a man, is able to work with Cardenio to advance her own interests. Lucinda spends most of the plot negotiating the limitations of her status as a noblewoman, for instance by passing secret letters. Like the light in the tower to which she is consistently compared (and that her name evokes), she is remote and contained. This is not to say that Lucinda is without agency, especially considering that the play opens with her pursuit of Cardenio. In her lines, she shows herself to be both passionate and clever, while in her decision to continue her relationship with Cardenio and in her kindness to Quixote, we see her independent thinking and open-mindedness. Yet Lucinda's agency is ironically limited by her class standing. Meanwhile, Dorotea spends most of her scenes outdoors and beyond gendered constraints, moving through several costume changes as she pretends to be a messenger boy and a forlorn princess. While Dorotea is clearly more vulnerable to the threats of the Marqués, Lucinda's station does not protect her from violence, as she is both nearly forced into marriage with and abducted by the Marqués.

The second complication is that nobility does not seem to promote any particular goodness or mercy in Lucinda's father, and while the Duke is no tyrant, his insistence on protocol (even hiding the infant son he conceived during an adulterous affair) is a far cry from the kindness and generosity of spirit that we see in Cardenio. A production may choose to push back on the role of class in this play by emphasizing Dorotea's agency and dignity, or the at times callous nature of other high-born characters in the play.

The third complication is the nature of the adaptation. In Cervantes's novel, Cardenio is born and raised as a nobleman, and he introduces himself to Quixote saying "my home, one of the finest cities in Andalucía; my family, noble; my parents, wealthy; my misfortune, so great that my parents had to weep and my family grieve" (Part I, 183). In the novel, Cardenio also loses Lucinda to a cruel romantic rival, Don Fernando, but prior to Fernando's treachery, there is no real obstacle to Lucinda and Cardenio's union, save that her father is greedy and too weak to resist Fernando's request. Unlike the play, the novel begins with the sequence in Act 3, where Quixote, Sancho, and the peasant meet the mad Cardenio and give him food in exchange for his sad tale. The play modifies this structure by leading with Cardenio and Lucinda's courtship and the difficulties posed by his status, which shifts the focus of the plot to the problems that class structure causes for romance. While Cardenio does turn out to be a nobleman by birth, the play raises the possibility that he is not in order to demonstrate the injustices of a system that allows men like the Marqués to manipulate the people around them.

About This Translation

The original text used for this translation is based on two editions of *Don Quijote de la Mancha*: Ignacio Arellano (2007) and Joan Oleza (1997). When encountering issues with either of these texts, we also consulted the 1621 edition of Castro's *Primera parte de las comedias de don Guillem de Castro*. Castro recreates the rich intertextuality of *Don Quixote* by weaving his adaptation with many of the same references found in the original novel; we have italicized any lines lifted directly from other texts to help highlight these moments. Finally, although the name of Cervantes's character is typically modernized as *Quijote* in Spanish, we have opted for the traditional spelling in the play text, as well as this introduction, as that is still the one most familiar to English-speaking audiences.

Our translation of *Don Quixote de la Mancha* was given two early staged readings that were invaluable for our process—by Red Bull Theater in October 2023, as part of our ongoing Hispanic Golden Age Classics collaborative series (http://www.redbulltheater.com/don-quixote), and by the Brown Bag Theatre Company/New Swan Shakespeare Center at the University of California, Irvine in November 2023.

RED BULL THEATER CAST
Duke: Keith Hamilton Cobb
Marques: Arturo Luis Soria
Cardenio: Darryl Gene Daughtry
Lisardo/Peasant: Luis Moreno
Lucinda: Irene Sofia Lucio
Teodoro/Priest: Zachary Fine
Dorotea: Ismenia Mendes
Fulgencio/Matron/Servant: Carol Halstead
Don Quixote: Jacob Ming-Trent
Sancho Panza: Carson Elrod
Maid/Servant: Melissa Mahoney

RED BULL PRODUCTION TEAM
Director: José Zayas
Stage Manager: Jenn McNeil
Video Coordinator: Jessica Fornear
Producing Director: Nathan Winkelstein
General Manager: Sherri Kotimsky

BROWN BAG THEATRE CAST
Narrator: Paulina Sofia Lugo Reyes
Cardenio/Squire: Bridgette Betanzos
Lucinda/Maid: Jasmine Cole
Dorotea: Evelyn Urusquieta
Marques: Armando Acosta
Duke/Priest/Matron: Jack Fowler
Lisardo/Teodoro/Servant: Aaron Bruce Gomez
Don Quixote/Hunter: Alonso Melgoza
Sancho Panza: Ethan Pante
Barber/Fideno/Fulgencio/Servant: Maia Lucas

BROWN BAG PRODUCTION TEAM
Directors: Eden Aztlán & Jesús López Vargas
Stage Manager: Sammie D. Moore
Illustrator: Destiny Esquivel
Lighting Designer: Kassia R. Curl
Assistant Lighting Designer: Rhea Remesh
Projections: Jesús López Vargas & Merle DeWitt III

References and Further Reading

Castro, Guillén de (1569-1631). *Primera parte de las comedias de Don Guillem de Castro*. 1621. https://gallica.bnf.fr/ark:/12148/bpt6k321223s/.

Castro, Guillén de. *Obras completas*. Ed. Joan Oleza. Fundación José Antonio de Castro, 1997.

Castro, Guillén de. *Comedia de Don Quixote de La Mancha. Don Quixote en el teatro español: del Siglo de Oro al siglo XX*. Ed. Ignacio Arellano. Visor Libros, 2007, 25–155.

Cervantes Saavedra, Miguel. *Don Quixote*. Trans. Edith Grossman. Ecco, 2003.

Pronunciation Guide

Each vowel in Spanish has just one sound. They are pronounced as follows:

a - AH
e - EH
i - EE
o - OH
u - OO

The <u>un</u>derlined <u>syll</u>able in each word is the <u>ac</u>cented one.

Marqués: MAHR-<u>KEHS</u>

Cardenio: CAHR-<u>DEH</u>-NEE-OH

Lisardo: LEE-<u>SAHR</u>-DOH

Lucinda: LOO-<u>SEEN</u>-DAH

Teodoro: TEH-OH-<u>DOH</u>-ROH

Dorotea: DOH-ROH-<u>TEH</u>-AH

Fideno: FEE-<u>DEH</u>-NOH

Fulgencio: FOOL-<u>HEN</u>-SEE-OH

Don Quixote: DOHN KEE-<u>HOH</u>-TEH

Sancho Panza: <u>SAHN</u>-CHOH <u>PAHN</u>-SAH

Amadís: AH-MAH-<u>DEES</u>

Babieca: BAH-<u>BYEH</u>-CA

Beltenebros: BEHL-TEHN-<u>EH</u>-BROHS

Characters:

DUKE
MARQUÉS, the Duke's son
CARDENIO, gentleman
LISARDO, Cardenio's father
LUCINDA, lady
TEODORO, Lucinda's father
DOROTEA, shepherdess
FIDENO, Dorotea's father
FULGENCIO
DON QUIXOTE
SANCHO PANZA
PRIEST
BARBER
MATRON
SQUIRE
MAID
PEASANT
HUNTERS (2 speaking roles)
SERVANTS (3 speaking roles; up to 6 roles total)

Doubling:

HUNTERS could double as SERVANTS

Any HUNTER or SERVANT could double as FIDENO, PEASANT, SQUIRE, PRIEST or BARBER

Any HUNTER or SERVANT could double as MATRON or MAID

LISARDO could double as SQUIRE

FIDENO or TEODORO could double as PEASANT, PRIEST or BARBER

Don Quixote de la Mancha

ACT I

SCENE 1

Hunting grounds

Enter Cardenio and Lucinda. She is dressed in hunting clothes with boots and spurs, and Cardenio helps her get up, as she has just fallen off a horse

Lucinda	Oh God!
Cardenio	That was close! You almost fell along with your horse. Hold on to me.
Lucinda	And so I find myself in your arms, saved from death's untimely embrace.
Cardenio	How did this come to pass, my lady? You are like that shining sun before which Phaeton's horses fell.[1]

---

1   In Greek mythology, Phaeton, son of Helios the sun god, steals his father's chariot, which carries the sun around the earth. Unable to control the horses, he crashes to earth.

I encountered you in a precarious state,
distressed and on the verge of falling,
yet rivaling the sun in your beauty,
gentle as a breeze.
I knew you by your noble attire,
as you came flying over the plain
and went hurtling toward the rocks.
Just before the horse tumbled to its death
in the valley below,
you leapt into my arms.
I must be dreaming.
To save a beauty such as yours
is the ultimate prize of love,
its greatest miracle.

LUCINDA The actual miracle is that you saved me
from the brink of death.
Now my gratitude will serve to justify my love.
I was in a small village on my father's estates
when I heard the Duke was out hunting with you.
I, too, decided to ride into the countryside.
Sometimes I go out alone,
for in the absence of one's beloved,
solitude is the best companion.
I heard the shouts of the hunting party
as they closed in on some wild beast.
If even men can't rein in their passions,
imagine how unbridled a woman might be,
especially one who sought to remedy her fortunes.
I was on my way to you, Cardenio,
almost mad with love.
As I spurred on my horse
towards the sound of the dogs,
his hooves became wings,
and when I tried to stop him,
he bucked and chomped at the bit.

>   As I tried to restrain him,
>   my hair came undone
>   and the wind took my veil.
>   Though I pulled on the reins,
>   he ran like the wind
>   and reared back like a demon. 50
>   As he reached this cliff,
>   unable to stop or turn,
>   he tumbled down into the valley.
>   I, too, would have fallen
>   had I not thrown myself into your arms.

CARDENIO   And so you became an angel
             fallen from heaven,
             though never cast from it.

LUCINDA   All this for...

CARDENIO   What, my lady? 60

LUCINDA   ...a silly wish...

CARDENIO   And have you fulfilled it?

LUCINDA   I'm not sure.

*LUCINDA looks around from one place to another,
as if suddenly cautious*

CARDENIO   What is it?
             Tell me.

LUCINDA   I feel...

CARDENIO   What has made you blush so?

LUCINDA (*Aside*) Dear heavens,
will the wind whisper my secrets?
Will the sun bring everything to light?
Will these pines shelter me as I speak to him,
when just one accusing finger
could cast a shadow over me?

CARDENIO What is there to fear
when your heart is true?
Speak freely.

LUCINDA Listen, by my life,
and if I am upset, forgive me.
It has been six long years
full of tender glances
since our eyes first declared
what our hearts could not contain.
For years I have wished
for a moment to speak to you alone,
so that I might unburden my heart,
free of shame and fear.
I never dared to say anything
when you came to my window.
Love gave me strength,
yet fear held me back.
Anyone can be bold from up high,
yet words become immodest
as they fall to the ground.
I could have put my cares to paper,
but they'd have been lost to the wind.
Now Heaven has given me a chance
to alleviate my sorrows and to speak,
though it may cost me dearly.
Tell me, Cardenio,
is it not true that at some point
men must act on their intentions?

| | And that those who speak of love
must intend marriage,
if not some other unfortunate arrangement
not worthy of mention?
You have been the world's most perfect suitor,
the most constant, the most wise,
the most caring and careful,
and I have responded in kind.
You have not suffered jealousy, 110
nor long absences from my side.
You have seen me at my window,
at mass, in my carriage...
I lose sleep over you at night
and all sense in the day...
What more do you desire
than to love and be loved,
to want and be wanted?
And yet this is how you respond,
to my eternal dismay. 120
Are those tears in your eyes
all you can muster? |
|---|---|
| CARDENIO | My lady, if only you knew
how many sighs I have swallowed,
how many tears I have shed,
how often love and honor
have battled within me! |
| LUCINDA | Why should that be?
(*Aside*) I can't take this! |
| CARDENIO | Oh my lovely Lucinda, 130
don't ask me these questions,
don't force me to answer. |
| LUCINDA | Am I not noble enough? |

CARDENIO You could be a king's own bride.

LUCINDA Or respectable?

CARDENIO Unparalleled.

LUCINDA Or wealthy?

CARDENIO More than enough.

LUCINDA What is it then?

CARDENIO It's my... 140

LUCINDA Are you married?

CARDENIO No, my lady.

LUCINDA Are you betrothed to another?

CARDENIO It's not that either.

LUCINDA Then tell me, what!

CARDENIO I am the unluckiest of men,
though Heaven knows I am honorable!

LUCINDA Is that a fault?

CARDENIO Yes, my lady,
for in these times
no honorable man 150
can be fortunate.
But listen, my lady,
I will tell you...

Enter DOROTEA, *shepherdess, running from the* MARQUÉS *as he grabs at her*

DOROTEA Stop following me!

MARQUÉS Wait!
Since when are you so fast?

DOROTEA escapes

DUKE (*Shouting from offstage*) Help!
Where is my son?

LUCINDA What is that?   160

DUKE (*Offstage*) Marqués, over here!
Help me, my son! Help!

MARQUÉS It's my father!

CARDENIO That's the Duke!

DUKE (*Offstage*) If only I were a younger man!

CARDENIO A bear has killed his horse!

CARDENIO tries to leave to aid the DUKE and is briefly held back by LUCINDA

LUCINDA Wait, Cardenio!

CARDENIO I cannot.

CARDENIO runs offstage

MARQUÉS (*Aside*) I am undone by love and fear.

	I will not go to him.	170
	I'll pretend...	

DUKE (*Offstage*) Oh heavens!

MARQUÉS (*Aside*) ...that I never heard him...

CARDENIO (*Offstage*) Away, you beast!

MARQUÉS (*Aside*) Why should I care
if death takes a father
who has already lived too long?

The MARQUÉS *exits.* LUCINDA *narrates how* CARDENIO *aids
the* DUKE *offstage*

LUCINDA God help you, Cardenio,
and keep you from harm.
What skill, what blows...   180
and what a victory!
He is a new Saint George,
with one foot on that beast,
terrifying even in death.
He is lifting the old Duke to his feet now.
and the Duke is embracing Cardenio.
They're coming this way.
I will hide here and wait.

LUCINDA *hides herself. Enter the* DUKE *and* CARDENIO,
who has injured his hand

DUKE My dear Cardenio,
this is why I've entrusted   190
my whole house to your good sense.
This is why I value your bravery above all others
and feel such deep and abiding love for you.

	I am much inclined toward one who does me so much good.
CARDENIO	You have made me what I am. I was born to serve you, and do so with all my soul.
DUKE	Let me take that victorious hand in mine... But you are injured! 200
CARDENIO	It's nothing, my lord.
LUCINDA	(*Aside*) Is that blood I see? Oh God!
DUKE	Show me.
CARDENIO	I just cut myself when I unsheathed my sword.
DUKE	Let me see...
CARDENIO	It's just a scratch, sir.
DUKE	And yet I feel as though it were my own blood. 210 I feel faint... Bandage it...
CARDENIO	I will.
DUKE	...it has such a strange effect on my heart.
LUCINDA	(*Aside*) And mine too!
DUKE	It pains me so,

	as if it flowed from my own veins.	

CARDENIO   I thank you from my very soul.

DUKE   And I would give my soul
to have given you life,   220
for then my estate and nobility
would pass down to one I love so well.

CARDENIO   Rejoice in the Marqués, my lord.
May the heavens keep him
a thousand years,
for he is your heir.

DUKE   That son of mine is a coward,
no mercy, no courage.
How could he be so cruel
and cowardly as to abandon me?   230
He saw how my horse collapsed on top of me,
yet did not come to my aid,
unstirred by my shouts for help,
unmoved in his uncaring depths,
untouched in his cowardly heart!

CARDENIO   My lord, I implore you to reconsider your words.
Had the Marqués heard your cries
he would have lent his whole soul to you,
and brought his sword to your aid.
Merciful is his nobility,   240
and strong is his steel.

DUKE   Oh, Cardenio!
My mind paints him
as a different sort entirely:
so incapable, so unjust,
so vulgar, so ungrateful,

| | so far from me in manner, |
| | so contrary to my taste...! |

CARDENIO   Spoken like a father.
             Wise fathers wish for such perfect sons   250
             that they can never measure up.
             Some of the Marqués's worst behaviors
             are just the foibles of youth.

DUKE   Madness and folly, you mean.

CARDENIO   All young men must sow their wild oats.
             Too much caution can be a great fault
             in a young man.

LUCINDA   (*Aside*) Oh, Cardenio!

DUKE   Your noble sentiments console me.
             Oh, heavens, if only I could exchange   260
             one nature for another!
             Proud and angry as I am,
             I wish that I could trade him for you.
             No man has ever had
             a son more reviled,
             nor a servant more beloved.

             Enter two of the DUKE's HUNTERS

HUNTER 1   Here is the Duke.
             Over here! Come!

HUNTER 2   Here, here!
             How slow they are!   270

DUKE   Here they are at last,
             now that the danger has passed.

	Yet none of them could keep up with me.	
Cardenio	Your horse just flew.	
Duke	They were close enough that they should have seen and heard me. Come, Cardenio, you can tend to your wound in my tent.	
Cardenio	It's just a scratch, my lord.	
Duke	Let's keep it that way.	280
Cardenio	(*Aside*) Oh, Lucinda! Where has she gone? I cannot leave the Duke... If only I could divide myself in two!	

Exit the Duke, Cardenio *and the* Hunters. Lucinda *remains alone on stage*

Lucinda	If only I could make him stay, or go be by his side! How I long to speak to him, how I pine for the sight of him! At least the tents are close by. Though I missed my chance once, I'll wait here for another, until I can satisfy the doubt that keeps holding me back.	290
Marqués	(*Offstage*) Surely a change of place must have brought a change of heart...	
Lucinda	I think I hear people. I must take cover.	

Lucinda hides. Enter the Marqués *and* Dorotea

DOROTEA   What do you want from me?

MARQUÉS   I'm mad for you.
           Stop, sweet girl, stop.   300
           You're mine now, my darling.
           Spare me your disdain.

DOROTEA   How can I, when I'm hunted down
           rather than won over?
           How can you do this…

MARQUÉS   Listen here, my lady.

DOROTEA   …to one of your own vassals?

MARQUÉS   Heaven knows how my soul longs for you.
           Calm down.

DOROTEA   I am calmer now.   310
           What do you want of me?

MARQUÉS   Consider how I burn for you,
           and how poorly you have rewarded my affection.
           Am I truly so hateful
           that you should torture me
           and prolong my suffering?
           You crush me with your denial
           and abandon me so easily.
           Now that I finally have you in my grasp,
           put me out of my misery: 320
           give me your answer once and for all.

DOROTEA   Even the most virtuous woman
           must respond to such courtesy.

Forgive my rudeness—
we country folk only let our anger show
when we have been much provoked.
If I have been too harsh,
it is not because your love leaves me cold.
Just because I am reserved
doesn't mean that your love tires me,   330
your looks displease me,
or your manner offends me.
Fleeing from you is another thing entirely
from rejecting you.
I flee from the sight of you
in order not to adore you.
Heaven knows that every bit of you
seems like heaven to me,
and I am so obliged
by everything that you are.   340
May I never have love
if I do not love you full well!
And yet I know my humble state,
and how low I am.
I see how high you are,
how close to majesty.
I am the daughter of a peasant,
rich though he may be,
and you are the eldest son
of a Spanish Grandee.[2]   350
I was born among cows and goats,
you were born from kings,
so how could you sully your blood with mine?
This is impossible, my lord.
I am an honorable woman,
and the honor of my body
sustains my very soul.

---

2   *Grandee*: The English term for "un Grande de España," an official aristocratic title for the highest nobility, such as dukes.

                I would rather lose that same soul
                than risk my spotless reputation
                for honor, honesty, and good sense.   360
                You must restrain yourself,
                as your own great worth
                deprives me of all good fortune.
                Know that this impossible distance
                frustrates me more than you.

MARQUÉS   Your virtue only whets my appetite.
                Your beauty captivates me
                and your words enchant me.
                I have all the more esteem
                for a woman with self-esteem.   370
                My sweet country girl,
                so near to my heart,
                you have no equal in all the world.
                Natural virtue is the greatest nobility of all.
                Even without your beauty,
                the King of Spain might love you
                and wed you for your virtue alone.
                Heaven is my witness,
                my soul is now yours
                and I give you my word   380
                that my hand will be, too.
                I must find satisfaction,
                even if it offends my nobility.
                Your blood may be rustic
                but it is still pure.
                Mine will take no taint from it.
                I would never marry one who did not please me.
                An unhappy marriage would be a waste
                of this most noble blood.
                Raise those starry eyes of yours, Dorotea, 390
                and look at me.
                I shall be yours,

>   you shall bear my children
>   and they will sustain my line,
>   for you will give them virtue,
>   and I, nobility.

DOROTEA   Do you mean it?

MARQUÉS   How can you doubt a love as great as mine?

DOROTEA   We country folk speak plainly, my lord.
           Your courtly truth comes so embellished   400
           with fine words and phrases
           that I can scarce recognize it.
           Still, though your intentions surprise me,
           such solid reasoning could not be built on lies.
           …And yet I cannot quite believe it.

MARQUÉS   Why do you doubt me?

DOROTEA   I am afraid.

MARQUÉS   You must believe me.

DOROTEA   I cannot believe that I deserve so much.

MARQUÉS   I swear by God above—   410

DOROTEA   Don't swear.

MARQUÉS   You're driving me mad!

DOROTEA   Let me think it over.
           And you, too, must give this more thought.
           Is that your father over there?
           Oh, this will be the end of me!

MARQUÉS	He has seen me— I must speak to him. But you must give me your word that you will not go.	420
DOROTEA	I give you my word.	
MARQUÉS	Hide yourself.	
DOROTEA	I'm overcome with fear.	
MARQUÉS	Why now? What bad timing!	

DOROTEA hides. Enter the DUKE with servants, and LISARDO,
an old peasant

LISARDO	My lord, I'm in search of your son and mine.	
DUKE	I love your son as much as my own. He is valiant and strong.	
LISARDO	(*Aside*) Just like his father.	
DUKE	There he is.	430
LISARDO	I'll go to him.	

Enter CARDENIO, as LUCINDA and DOROTEA stay separately hidden
to the either side. The MARQUÉS kisses the DUKE's hand.
The DUKE then paces back and forth, observing him

CARDENIO	(*Aside*) Where is the light of my life?
LUCINDA	(*Aside*) I want to go to Cardenio.

DOROTEA (*Aside*) I am quaking with fear.

LUCINDA (*Aside*) But who is that peasant with him?

LISARDO My son!

LUCINDA (*Aside*) His son?

CARDENIO Father.

LUCINDA (*Aside*) He called him father,
and kissed his hand. 440
Either I am dreaming,
or this will be the end of me.
If that is Cardenio's father,
then that would explain
why he has always been
so hesitant, so timid.

DOROTEA (*Aside*) The Duke doesn't seem very pleased to see his son!

MARQUÉS (*Aside*) How he glares at me.
He must know I neglected my duty.

DUKE (*To* MARQUÉS) So, my lord… 450

MARQUÉS (*Aloud*) My lord…
(*Aside*) This is the calm before the storm.

LUCINDA (*Aside*) Who have I fallen for?
Who is this Cardenio, who consumes my soul?

CARDENIO (*To* LISARDO) Dear father, you should return home now.

DUKE	(*To* MARQUÉS) How was the hunt for you?
	Did you kill many wild beasts?
	I'm sure they all fled before you.
MARQUÉS	I couldn't quite catch them.
DUKE	It is hard to kill anything 460
	when you're so afraid of dying.
LISARDO	(*To* CARDENIO) Goodbye, then.

LISARDO exits

CARDENIO	Godspeed, father.
LUCINDA	(*Aside*) Dear God!
	What shall I do?
CARDENIO	How unfortunate!
	(*Aside*) Oh Lucinda, now you see with your own
	eyes what my words could not convey.
	I am ashamed.
MARQUÉS	(*Aside*) That was a low blow. 470
DUKE	Honorable men tend to duty
	before pleasure.
CARDENIO	(*He spots* LUCINDA) There she is.
DOROTEA	(*Aside*) I am so afraid!
	What a state the Duke is in!
	How he paces back and forth!
	Ten steps and barely a word!
MARQUÉS	(*Aloud*) What is my offense, my lord?

Cardenio	(*Aside to* Lucinda) Ah, my lady, must you sigh so? You seem very different now!	480
Duke	You have not been at my table. Is my health not your concern? Is it not your place to care for me in my old age?	
Marqués	My lord...	
Duke	Should you not be there attending to me, cutting up my meat so that I might eat?	
Dorotea	(*Aside*) I am shaking at the sound of this.	490
Marqués	I have been delayed through no fault of my own.	
Duke	But of course you could not do that, for fear the knife might nick you.	
Marqués	Oh God!	
Cardenio	(*To* Lucinda) If you weep now in disappointment, what would you have done had I encouraged you all along? That is why, though you thought me a gentleman up high on my horse, I tried valiantly to rein it in. While your favors brightened my dress and gave new wings to my heart, I knew I could only aspire to what you are, given what I am.	500

	I was frozen in my daring,
	though warmed by your fire.
	Forgive me.
	And if what has happened between us offends you, 510
	I will bury myself in those fields,
	tended by the father who sired me.

DUKE   Well, eat up now, Marqués.
          Perhaps your valor will be nourished
          by the beast that Cardenio slew.

Exit the DUKE and his servants, then enter LISARDO

LISARDO   (*To MARQUÉS*) Give me your hand, my son.

MARQUÉS   I wish I were your son,
          then I would not resent
          this low treatment.

LISARDO   (*Aside*) Ay, my dear boy!   520

MARQUÉS   Forgive me, Lisardo.
          Leave me now.

LISARDO   May God be with you.

LISARDO exits. DOROTEA and LUCINDA emerge from their hiding places. DOROTEA speaks to the MARQUÉS on one side, and LUCINDA speaks to CARDENIO on the other

DOROTEA   (*To MARQUÉS*) Thank God they've gone.

MARQUÉS   You gave me your word…

DOROTEA   And I've kept my word.
          I only promised to wait.

CARDENIO (*To LUCINDA*) Speak to me,
or if your anger is too fierce,
kill me with this steel. 530

CARDENIO kneels and offers his dagger to LUCINDA

LUCINDA If I were as fierce as you claim,
I wouldn't hesitate.
But no, rise so that I may
favor you with my love.
I owe you my life
and offer my soul in exchange.
Had I known of your humble birth from the start
I would have blamed myself
for loving you so freely.
Yet since I was deceived 540
and have loved you for so long,
to stop now would solve nothing.
And so, no matter what people might say,
for better or for worse,
for richer or poorer,
I'll have you as you are.
Though you are born of these fields,
you shall be mine
and I shall be yours.
Do not blame me for doubting and weeping, 550
these are but honorable misgivings.
Though I wish I could change
the nature of your birth,
I will not leave you over it.

CARDENIO And I will worship the ground you walk on.

LUCINDA If only I could enjoy this love,
without feeling such apprehension.

Exit LUCINDA and CARDENIO

DOROTEA   Let me go.

MARQUÉS   By God, don't make this difficult.

DOROTEA   You've already asked too much,　　　　560
and I've given more than enough.
Your love compelled me to give in,
until I saw your father the Duke.
That noble reserve,
that stern reproach,
that prideful heart,
that harsh demeanor,
that fierce expression,
that unbridled anger,
that scolding gaze!　　　　570
He paced back and forth,
surveying all who serve him,
every last one dreading him,
and trembling before him.
The sight of him commanding
a thousand men—
they doff their hats,
and he bites off their heads.
The sight of him greeting you—
he did not take you in his arms　　　　580
but instead looked ready to swallow you whole.
It scared me to death.
If this is what it means to be a noble,
I would rather remain humble.
Leave me to my shepherds
and our coarse speech,
as we talk about goats, and lambs,
and other small things.
Leave me to the hunt,

                where my aim is true, 590
where I need not fear
missing the mark.
I always return home
with a quail or a hare,
to feed my aging father
with what I have caught myself.
There he receives me
with open arms.
His embrace is worth more to me
than the whole world. 600
I must reject your offer
though it makes me weep.
I do this for you,
not because I don't love you,
not because I don't adore you.
Though my position is low,
I prize it as my own.
Your nobility overwhelms me.
If I could only make you a peasant
rather than have you make me a lady! 610
I must go.

MARQUÉS   This is how you leave me?

                He grabs her hand

DOROTEA   Let go of my hand, Marqués.

MARQUÉS   You won't leave here
                without promising to be mine.

DOROTEA   Let me go.

MARQUÉS   You're killing me.
                Wait.

DOROTEA	I will not wait, for if I pause to look at you I will never go. Let go of me.	620
MARQUÉS	How can you do this? I can treat you like a peasant if that's what you want. I will find some release one way or another!	
DOROTEA	I will scream to high heaven so all the world may hear!	

DON QUIXOTE yells from offstage

DON QUIXOTE	Pick up the pace! I hear a damsel in distress. Onward, Sancho, onward!³ I'll show you what it means to be a knight-errant!	630

Enter DON QUIXOTE astride Rocinante, dressed just as described in the book

	I shall first dismount. I do not wish to attack with an unfair advantage. Whoa, Rocinante! (*To MARQUÉS*) Dost thou dare harm such a beautiful maiden? Away from her, knight-erroneous!	640
MARQUÉS	Must I face a madman now,	

---

3   Line taken directly from a traditional Spanish ballad: "Corre, Sancho, ataja, ataja"

| | when I too am on the brink of madness? |
| | Leave us. |

DON QUIXOTE You are a lout,
             unworthy of the name of knight!

DOROTEA   Such a noble defender!
             I would laugh were I not crying.

MARQUÉS   I might enjoy this madness,
             were I not mad for love.   650

DON QUIXOTE I am a knight-errant,
             equal to the best of them—
             Amadís, Don Belianís, and the Knight of Febo—[4]
             and you have angered me.
             I seek adventure to avenge all wrongs,
             and now I must avenge that lip of yours
             whence such nonsense hath spilled.

MARQUÉS   Watch yourself,
             I have my men with me.

DON QUIXOTE As the famed Agrajes once said: 660
             I'll show you![5]
             Draw thy sword, scoundrel,
             while I, like a true Spaniard,
             shall cleave the sun in twain.

DOROTEA   Protect yourself from this madman, my lord!

---

    4   *Amadís, Don Belianís, Knight of Febo*: Central characters in popular 16th-century chivalric romances *Amadís of Gaul*, *Belianís of Greece* (a continuation of *Amadís*), and *The Knight of Febo*.

    5   *Agrajes*: Cousin of the famous knight Amadís, he appears in the first installment of Amadís's story, eventually becoming King of Scotland and fodder for the sequels.

MARQUÉS   Even the fools are after me!
             Let him have it, men!

DOROTEA exits. Enter the MARQUÉS's servants with clubs who chase DON QUIXOTE

DON QUIXOTE Steady there, you ruffians.
             How dare you attack me,
             you who are not knights?   670

MARQUÉS   (*Calls to DOROTEA offstage*)
             Don't run too far on those pretty little feet.
             My love will find you in the end!

Exit the MARQUÉS and his servants, leaving DON QUIXOTE on the ground

DON QUIXOTE You have offended knighthood itself,
             but my sword shall return
             to punish your low villainy.
             You have slain me, savage giant,
             with your giant club.
             Oh, beloved Dulcinea,
             you alone can aid your gallant knight
             in such straits!   680

DUKE   (*From offstage*) Who shouts there?
             Servants, where is the Marqués!

Enter the DUKE and three SERVANTS

SERVANT 1   My lord, the Marqués is gone.

DUKE   After him!

SERVANT 2   And he has three men with him.

DUKE   We must go after them.

SERVANT 3   This way! They're over there!

DON QUIXOTE   Oh, cruel Don Carloto!⁶

Exit the DUKE *and his* SERVANTS. *Enter* SANCHO PANZA

SANCHO   What a ruckus!
               To risk my life, for this!   690
               Where can I take cover, Don Quixote, sir?
               Help, lend me your courage!
               I'm at death's door.

DON QUIXOTE   *Where canst thou be, oh lady mine,*
               *that by my plight thou art not moved?*⁷

SANCHO   Who are you saying such nonsense to?

DON QUIXOTE   *Once thou didst take to heart*
               the smallest e'en of my wounds.

SANCHO   Damn the one who wounded you!

DON QUIXOTE   Dry thy tears, faithful squire of mine.   700

SANCHO   Oh, Don Quixote! This is killing me!

DON QUIXOTE   I am not Don Quixote.

---

6   *Don Carloto*: Son of Charlemagne and the villain from the *Ballad of the Marqués of Mantua, Which Tells How the Marqués Came Upon His Nephew on His Way Home, Mortally Wounded by the Prince Don Carloto...* the full title of which explains the plot of the poem.

7   The lines in italics are taken directly from Chapter 5 of Cervantes's novel. Our translation uses the lines from the Cervantes Project's Varorium Edition: http://cervantes.tamu.edu/V2/CPI/TEI/TEI_1605/1605/1605/chapter5.html

	I am nephew to my lord of Mantua,
	who followed the hunt
	to the shores of the sea.
	I am Lord Valdovinos.[8]

SANCHO   Well, you look like Don Quixote to me,
            though it's true you've looked better.

DON QUIXOTE You just don't understand!
            Haven't I told you   710
            this is what knight errancy is all about?
            Enchantments abound!
            A mere frog, or some such creature,
            might become a giant one moment
            and a tortoise the next.
            And so, though I was Don Quixote
            when hale and hearty,
            once those malevolent clubs
            cast their spell on me,
            I became the wounded Valdovinos.   720
            Can't you see the woods,
            thick with brambles and thorns?
            Can't you see the oak trees and boulders,
            and me sprawled on the ground?
            Can't you see my mortal wounds?
            Didn't you hear me say:
            "Where canst thou be, oh lady mine,
            that by my plight thou art not moved?"
            If that was me and I said that,
            what halfwit wouldn't believe   730
            that I am Valdovinos?

SANCHO   You're right.
            I must have confused myself.

---

    8   *Valdovinos*: The aforementioned grievously wounded nephew from the *Ballad of the Marqués of Mantua*.

DON QUIXOTE   Exactly, you fool.

SANCHO   So who am I then?

DON QUIXOTE   The squire to this poor,
   ill-fated prince.

SANCHO   I will weep for you, Valdovinos, sir.

DON QUIXOTE   Go fetch me a priest
   to hear my confession.   740

Enter the PRIEST and the BARBER, who have been searching for DON QUIXOTE

SANCHO   I'll go at once,
   though I hate to do so…
   Wait, isn't that the Barber and the Priest?
   What a stroke of luck!
   Here they come to cure you
   and hear your confession.

PRIEST   This is a strange scene.

BARBER   Strange indeed.
   (*To SANCHO*) Where is your master?

SANCHO   He's injured,   750
   and he's actually Valdovinos now.

DON QUIXOTE   Where is the good hermit
   who will confess me?

PRIEST   Is this what your nonsense
   has led you to, Quijada?

DON QUIXOTE *Oh, cousin Montesinos!*
            Oh, Prince Merián![9]

            Enter the DUKE and the SERVANTS

SERVANT 1   The Marqués ordered us to…

DUKE   It was not right of him to do so.
            Is this the man you beat?   760

SERVANT 2   Get back, sir, get back!
            This man is mad.

DUKE   Well, if he's mad,
            why did they hurt him so?
            Where did he come from?
            Who is he?

DON QUIXOTE I am of Mantua, noble Marqués,
            and you my mother's brother, no less!

DUKE   God help us!

BARBER   You are right to wonder   770
            about the state he's in.
            Yet I can explain the cause
            if you'll listen.

DON QUIXOTE Don Carloto has treacherously slain me
            for the hand of my fair wife.
            The beautiful princess Sevilla
            is the cause of all this strife.

---

9   *Montesinos, Prince Merián*: Lines taken directly from the Valdovinos ballad, "Oh mi primo Montesinos, Infante don Merín, desecha es la compañía en que solíamos andar!" (line 104).

PRIEST	Would you like to confess then,
	Valdovinos, as you're on your deathbed?
DUKE	(*Playing along*) Yes, do so, oh son of my sister. 780
DON QUIXOTE	Good hermit, approach.
DUKE	I do not know whether to laugh or cry.
DON QUIXOTE	I confess…
PRIEST	Go on, but quietly.
DON QUIXOTE	Give me a moment.
BARBER	This gentleman, though poor,
	is from an old family of La Mancha.
	His solitude and misfortune
	sadly led him to read
	morning, noon and night. 790
	His books are full of nonsense:
	ships travel on land,
	and mountains cross the seas.
	A single blow slices through
	the necks of ten giants
	whose blood floods the earth.
	And all of it to save damsels in distress.
DON QUIXOTE	I confess—as I was saying—
	that I was slow to come to the aid
	of a fair maiden… 800
PRIEST	That's very bad!
	Don't do it again.
BARBER	And so, he lost his wits

                and came to believe
                all those terrible feats of chivalry were true.
                Fully out of his mind,
                he dusted off the breastplate and armor
                that had belonged to his grandfather,
                and donned a helmet—
                which fits him about as well as you can see.   810
                He took this peasant,
                as coarse as he is simple, as his squire,
                then had him saddle an old workhorse,
                all skin and bones, as his mighty steed.
                Thus armed, he rode from our village.
                The Priest and I followed him,
                out of pity and friendship.

DON QUIXOTE   And also, I was cowed by a fierce giant
                and tried to run away—
                though I did kill him later.   820

PRIEST   Next time, don't let him cow you.

BARBER   He went in search of adventures,
                forgetting that you need not look for trouble—
                it will find you.
                His name is Quijada,
                and he is Manchegan by birth,
                so he calls himself
                Don Quixote de la Mancha.
                The horse he calls Rocinante,
                all to imitate the chivalric order   830
                that has scrambled his brains.

DON QUIXOTE   Also, I longed to take revenge
                for the beatings they gave me...

PRIEST   Do you forgive them now?

DON QUIXOTE   Yes, I forgive them,
              though it's hard.

PRIEST   As penance, you must return
              to your house, and not ever leave it
              without my permission.

DON QUIXOTE   I will do as you say.   840

PRIEST   (*To DUKE*) Indulging a madman
              can on occasion cure him.

DUKE   This is the strangest thing I've ever seen.
              Someone should burn those books!

PRIEST   I just did.

DUKE   You've done well to avenge
              this attack on the truth.

DON QUIXOTE   Embrace me now, dear uncle,
              and pass that embrace on to my wife.
              Will you do that for a dying man?   850

DUKE   (*To DON QUIXOTE*) Yes, nephew.
              (*To PRIEST*) Have you ever seen the like?
              Let's take him to my tent
              where he might be cured
              if not of his madness, at least of his wounds.
              (*To SERVANTS*) You there, carry him in!

SANCHO   Sir?

DON QUIXOTE   Oh, my good squire,
              I've been beaten on the pate!
              Ermelinda, noble queen,   860

your son is in such a state!
Oh, Sevilla, princess mine,
as I go to my grave I say
we shall not see one another
until the judgment day!

*Servants carry Don Quixote offstage,
Duke, Priest, Barber, and Sancho follow*

End of Act I

ACT II
SCENE 1

A room in the palace

Enter MARQUÉS and a SERVANT, with MARQUÉS tearing up a letter

MARQUÉS	Who could believe this!
	And yet why am I surprised?
	When women hate you,
	they persist in their disdain.
	Yet it's even worse 870
	when they pester you with their love.
	Why won't this shepherdess leave me alone?
SERVANT	She claims you deceived her.
MARQUÉS	It's all part of the chase.
SERVANT	She sighs tenderly and weeps bitter tears.
	Her cries ring through the fields and plains.
	Her eyes proclaim her sorrows
	as she wrings her fair hands.
	Torn between patience and anger,
	she clasps them over her heart. 880
MARQUÉS	I care not.
	There is another woman now

who has taken her place in my heart.

Servant exits as Cardenio enters

You, Cardenio!

CARDENIO   My lord?

MARQUÉS   I need your counsel and your assistance.

CARDENIO   My life and my honor
are at your service.

MARQUÉS   I'm sure you know how Dorotea
once disdained my love.   890

CARDENIO   I know it well.

MARQUÉS   And you know how a man burns
amid the flames of desire.
Consumed by those flames,
I gave Dorotea my word
that I would be her husband.
With these assurances,
she gave in to my advances.
No sooner had I enjoyed her,
than I left her and despised her.   900

CARDENIO   That is often the way
with a love based on lust.

MARQUÉS   It was easy to move on.
I'm dying now for another lady,
whose favor I seek.
The love of these two
keeps me up at night.

>   One refuses my favors with tender excuses,
>   while the other hounds me ceaselessly.
>   But you will bring me relief! 910
>   You will help me with the first problem
>   and advise me on the second.

CARDENIO   You know you can ask anything of me...
            (*Aside*) ...although I fear it will be my undoing.

MARQUÉS   What do I have to lose
            by not keeping my word?

CARDENIO   My lord, a man's honor
            is based on his word.
            He must always keep it,
            lest he tarnish and stain his reputation. 920
            When a man doesn't keep his word,
            that shows it was not given in good faith.

MARQUÉS   What if keeping his word
            is the very thing that tarnishes his honor,
            isn't that an excuse?

CARDENIO   He should have considered that
            before making his promise.

MARQUÉS   And if he didn't?

CARDENIO   The code of honor is very strict on this point.

MARQUÉS   Must I marry a peasant then? 930

CARDENIO   No, not that, God forbid.

MARQUÉS   What can I do then
            in this awful fix?

CARDENIO	Don't be alarmed. Where there's a will there's a way, even if things seem grim. Although Dorotea is a country girl, her father has a fine estate. He spins his wool, his oil, his cheese, his wine into great heaps of gold. 940 His vast lands produce wheat by the bushel, honey by the barrel, and pastures full of cattle. When the father dies, she'll inherit the entire estate. None of this would matter if she were not beautiful, but since she is, it shouldn't be hard for you 950 to find her a fitting husband. Once you have put this to her, she will gladly release you from your promise, and then you will be at ease.
MARQUÉS	I'm very grateful for this advice, Cardenio, and much obliged to you. And as there is no one I love more, I want you to have the pleasure of all that beauty and all that gold. 960 My Cardenio, you will be the one to spend this treasure and enjoy this woman.
CARDENIO	What? (*Aside*) I have no words.
MARQUÉS	(*Aside*) He must be offended.

                    He holds himself so highly.
                    (*Aloud*) You have nothing to say?

CARDENIO   (*Aloud*) My silence is my response.

MARQUÉS   What's the matter?   970

CARDENIO   I cannot believe you treat me this way.
                    You nursed at the breast
                    of the mother who bore me.
                    For twelve years we lived together as brothers
                    in a peasant's cottage.
                    I've been your faithful servant all these years,
                    but you seem to think I have no honor
                    because of my low birth.
                    Would that I had never been born at all!
                    My low station is God's doing.   980
                    If it were up to me,
                    I would be second to no man.
                    Though it may cost my life,
                    I must make this clear:
                    I am an honorable man.
                    The nobility I have earned
                    is as dear to me
                    as the one you claim by birth.
                    Your example even now
                    spurs me on to seek virtue.   990
                    Neither heat nor light
                    can spin gold out of dishonor.
                    Forgive me for getting carried away.

MARQUÉS   How can I blame you
                    for your honorable thoughts?
                    You must forgive me for trying
                    to offer you what is mine.
                    When I heard how you praised her

| | and how you extoled her estate,
I thought that you wanted her for yourself. 1000
I'll find another man to marry her,
and so secure the freedom
to pursue that other angel instead. |
|---|---|
| CARDENIO | (*Aside*) Another bitter pill to swallow. |
| MARQUÉS | Cardenio, the woman I love
is beautiful, rich, and noble,
chaste, and refined. |
| CARDENIO | Is she your equal? |
| MARQUÉS | Not quite my rank... |
| CARDENIO | Who is she? 1010
(*Aside*) Do I even want to know? |
| MARQUÉS | ...but equal in nobility. |
| CARDENIO | (*Aside*) How can I stand this?
I'm sure I know! |

Enter LUCINDA *with attendants accompanying her*

| MARQUÉS | Here she is before me,
dazzling in her beauty. |
|---|---|
| CARDENIO | (*Aside*) What's this I see?
Am I dreaming?
My blood freezes over.
Some spell has turned me to stone. 1020
But no, I would not feel so strongly if that were so. |
| MARQUÉS | Isn't she beautiful? Isn't she a miracle to behold? |

LUCINDA (*Aside*) This will be the death of me.
Why is this happening to me?

CARDENIO (*Aside*) I am the most miserable man!

MARQUÉS She is the most beautiful woman!

LUCINDA (*Aside*) Cardenio and the Marqués, here!
My pain and my glory:
one will be the death of me
and the other is my life. 1030
How sad Cardenio looks, how distressed!
Does he know,
has he learned of my misfortune?

CARDENIO (*Aside*) My sorrows rain down upon me,
I can't help but weep.

The MARQUÉS offers his arm to LUCINDA as though to walk off with her

LUCINDA I will go no further.

MARQUÉS I cannot leave you here by yourself.

LUCINDA It's not my place to walk by your side.
Cardenio is enough for me.

MARQUÉS (*Aside*) So she loves him. 1040

CARDENIO (*Aside*) Oh, music to my ears!

MARQUÉS (*Aside*) Women never know what's best for them.

LUCINDA pretends to stumble. She holds onto CARDENIO and passes him a handkerchief with a note inside

LUCINDA	Goodness!
MARQUÉS	Have you fallen?
LUCINDA	I can't imagine how.
MARQUÉS	The path seems fairly clear to me.
LUCINDA	My sorrows are a stumbling block.
CARDENIO	(*Aside*) And my misery is a mountain.
MARQUÉS	I see nothing to stumble on here.
LUCINDA	It is my own weakness. 1050
MARQUÉS	Any woman who falls so readily must wish to do so.
LUCINDA	I don't fall that readily. If I cared to fall, I am not the kind of woman who'd just trip on her heels. But though I'm light on my feet, my cares weigh me down. If I do stumble, it is over weighty things, 1060 and I fully see the cause.
MARQUÉS	You are so careful in your falling, but don't forget to account for your honor, and consider what this could cost you.
LUCINDA	Since my honor depends on it, I will.
CARDENIO	(*Aside*) All my woes are numbered here.

LUCINDA   (*Aside*) Oh lord!

MARQUÉS   You shouldn't ask to stay here.

LUCINDA   And you shouldn't insist on taking me away.

MARQUÉS   Let Cardenio stay, and come with me.   1070
               I will be sure to catch you
               if you trip again.

The MARQUÉS and LUCINDA exit, leaving CARDENIO alone

CARDENIO   Oh heavens, how I have fallen!
               I was over the moon,
               and where am I now?
               I never stumbled,
               yet Fortune has struck me down.
               Lucinda, where will this lead?
               So much doubt, confusion, uncertainty!
               You were right to leave me this,   1080
               for you knew that I would weep.

CARDENIO examines the handkerchief

               But wait, there is a letter tied inside it!
               My sorrow, though deep,
               is no longer as piercing.
               May this untie the knot
               that lingers in my throat.

CARDENIO reads the letter

               "As you know, the Marqués has been relentless in his
               pursuit of me. Now he has spoken to my father and I
               am forced to go with him. In order to let you know, I
               asked to say goodbye to his mother as an excuse   1090

to give you this message.
At least this letter remains yours, since I cannot.
Lucinda."

What is this curse that plagues me?
My heart breaks
and I long for death.
What then is left to dread?
What could be worse
than waiting here,
in the wake of this? 1100
My soul, filled with sorrow,
has no room left for fear.
I shall face the storm.

The MARQUÉS enters

MARQUÉS Ah there you are, Cardenio.

CARDENIO (*Aside*) I cannot bear to look upon him!

MARQUÉS Now you know the object of my desire.
I have a task for you.

CARDENIO Sir, my duty requires me
to serve you most loyally
and never deceive you. 1110
The woman you claim to love,
that vision, that beauty,
once all my happiness,
is now my misfortune,
and will be the death of me.
Though I have adored her for six years,
and for five she has loved me in return,
given my low station,
I never proposed,

weeping instead for my misfortune.　　　　　1120
When my humble upbringing
was finally revealed,
to my delight she overcame her doubts
and promised to be my wife.
My lord, now that you know this,
if you still want a wife
who has pledged herself to me,
I will go and leave you
to take the place that would be mine
were I a luckier man.　　　　　1130
I will go where sorrow
will surely be the end of me—
to the mountains for some beast to devour,
or to the sea for some creature to swallow.
Or you could kill me yourself,
and turn cold the blood
that once burned for her.

CARDENIO gets down on his knees

MARQUÉS　　Rise, upon my life.
I suspected some of this,
but did not know the whole truth.　　　　　1140

CARDENIO　　If you read this,
you will understand why I weep.

CARDENIO gives the MARQUÉS the letter

MARQUÉS　　(*Aside*) A peasant must not enjoy
what my own soul desires,
even if I must kill him myself.

The MARQUÉS reads the letter to himself silently

CARDENIO	(*Aside*) Guide his heart, oh Heavens, and remedy my pain. Let him recognize the truth of my claim.
MARQUÉS	(*Aside*) How could one so lowly deserve a woman so beautiful? 1150 Why has he been blessed with such a lucky star? My sword is eager to cut his fortune short. But no, I will steal his blessing through deceit instead. (*Aloud*) Two men raised as brothers owe each other certain courtesies. It would be unthinkable for me to learn of this and not act. You must have Lucinda, 1160 and in case her father refuses you, I will tell you what I have planned.
CARDENIO	Let me kiss your feet, or at least the ground they walk upon.
MARQUÉS	Rise.

The MARQUÉS offers his hand to help CARDENIO up

CARDENIO	I am not worthy of your hand…
MARQUÉS	Rise, I say. (*Aside*) All the better to knock you down again. (*Aloud*) Come, I'll explain.
CARDENIO	Sir, your nobility has given me new life. 1170 (*Aside*) Oh fickle Fortune, mend your ways to match my steady heart!

The MARQUÉS and CARDENIO exit

SCENE 2

Outside DOROTEA's home

Enter DOROTEA alone, in her garden

DOROTEA   When shall I find peace at last?
I search for it everywhere,
yet it is nowhere to be found.
Cruel Marqués, you will be the death of me!
If only you had left me alone!
But you wouldn't let me be,
and now you've left me like this.   1180
Can such love turn to disdain?
Can such care turn to neglect?
Is this how a nobleman behaves?
Were you born to such things?

DOROTEA goes to sit by a fountain

Green meadow, clear fountain,
grant me repose
and a mirror for my tears.
But stop—I cannot bear
to look upon my own shame.
And yet I can't look away,   1190
for the tears on my face
reflect my heartbreak.

Enter DON QUIXOTE and SANCHO

DON QUIXOTE   We've arrived at a castle.

SANCHO	A house, you mean.
DON QUIXOTE	Nonsense! By the knighthood I profess, I swear this place is enchanted. See those gates adorned with imperial arms! Its master must hold himself 1200 in high esteem.
SANCHO	Those are just rabbit skins hung up to dry!
DON QUIXOTE	No, those are clearly the eagles of Greece. And this is just a side gate! All around are green meadows, beautiful fountains, and a maiden.
DOROTEA	Traitor, why couldn't you just leave me alone?
DON QUIXOTE	She lays upon the meadow and weeps away her sorrow. See how she reclines 1210 at the edge of the fountain. The sun hath never seen such loveliness.
DOROTEA	What agony!
DON QUIXOTE	By my faith as a knight-errant, what a mighty adventure we have here! She weeps crystals and pearls over cheeks of snow and roses. If she is not the sun, she is at least the dawn, 1220 which is the herald of the sun.

SANCHO   For God's sake, let's just get out of here!

DON QUIXOTE   Hush, Sancho!

SANCHO   The only thing she heralds
                 is another beating like the one
                 that turned you into Valdovinos last time.

DON QUIXOTE   Thus you forsake me, you dolt?
                 Where would you be safer
                 than by my side?

SANCHO   I'd rather be a chicken   1230
                 than a beaten egg.

DON QUIXOTE   Quiet, you fool, and look there,
                 if you have the courage:
                 a chariot approaches,
                 drawn by two steeds.
                 Do you see it?

SANCHO   I do.

DON QUIXOTE   Do you see the dwarf that leads them
                 with a whip, and how ugly he is?

SANCHO   I see a boy driving a mule and a cart.   1240

DON QUIXOTE   You and your peasant eyes.
                 Don't you see an old man on horseback
                 with his squire?

SANCHO   By God, I do.

DON QUIXOTE   And another squire on foot,
                 leading a horse by the reins,

	and others there on their mules?
Sancho	Sure.
Don Quixote	Now you'll see the strength of my arms. No doubt some knight-errant 1250 has been wounded or killed. My fearless courage will not stand for it.
Sancho	They've stopped, sir.
Don Quixote	And right at this castle's gate!

Fideno, Dorotea's father, calling from inside

Fideno	(*Offstage*) Dorotea! My daughter!
Dorotea	Heavens! My father is calling me.
Fideno	(*Offstage*) Dorotea!
Dorotea	I cannot even suffer in peace! 1260

Exit Dorotea

Sancho	Look, the carriage has burst open like a ripe fruit.

Lucinda, her father Teodoro, and their Servants exit from a carriage in the distance, while Don Quixote and Sancho describe the scene

Don Quixote	And inside there is a damsel in distress.

SANCHO   She seems fine to me.
                The old man is dismounting.

DON QUIXOTE   I see now what this is.
                That wicked sorcerer
                must have put her under a spell
                to whisk her away to this castle.

SANCHO   What a dastardly deed!   1270

DON QUIXOTE   Oh chivalry,
                what visions you visit upon me!

SANCHO   See how she weeps
                as they lead her inside.

DON QUIXOTE   The lord of the castle
                receives her at the gate.

SANCHO   And the old man now returns to his horse.

DON QUIXOTE   Is it a griffin,
                or maybe the famous hippogryph?[10]
                Don't you see how he flies away   1280
                through the air on his winged steed,
                as it spews thick smoke from its nostrils?

SANCHO   That's a trot at most...

DON QUIXOTE   Don't be silly.
                Can't you see it has a comet on its brow
                and a lightning bolt for a tail
                to help it fly?

---

10 *Hippogryph*: In Ludovico Ariosto's epic poem *Orlando furioso* (c. 1516), a flying creature half eagle, half horse that the knight Astolfo rides across continents and to the Moon.

SANCHO	And below its tail, what do you see there?[11]
DON QUIXOTE	Are you mad? There's nothing there.
SANCHO	Yeah, that's what I've been saying.
DON QUIXOTE	Someday you will see the truth which is granted only to ordained knights.
SANCHO	So the old man flew away on his griffin?
DON QUIXOTE	And the maiden that we saw being led into the castle has come out again.

Enter LUCINDA in traveling clothes, with DOROTEA, FIDENO, and servants

FIDENO	You'll feel better with some fresh air.
DON QUIXOTE	(*To SANCHO*) What a marvelous adventure! Now you'll see how mad I can be!
SANCHO	Watch out, there's the old wizard.
LUCINDA	I don't care where I go.
DOROTEA	You seem so sad.

LUCINDA speaks aside privately to a SERVANT

LUCINDA	Wait for him on the road

---

[11] He is making a dirty joke about the horse being gelded.

	and bring him here.	
SERVANT	Yes, my lady.	

Exit SERVANT

FIDENO	I am sorry that your father left in such a rush.	
LUCINDA	(*Aside*) He is in a hurry to deliver me to my death. (*Aloud*) The journey made me ill… (*Aside*) If only it had killed me! (*Aloud*) …and I had to stop at your house.	1310
FIDENO	My household is at your service.	
LUCINDA	God be with you.	
DOROTEA	My lady, what is troubling you?	
LUCINDA	I would tell you if we were alone.	
DON QUIXOTE	That's my cue!	1320

DON QUIXOTE *pops out*

LUCINDA	Jesus, what an odd sight!
DON QUIXOTE	Hath your fair ladyship perchance suffered some fell misdeed?
LUCINDA	What a laughable figure!
DOROTEA	Laughter often comes

	in the midst of tears.	
DON QUIXOTE	Staunch your tears a while,	
	and tell me,	
	as one who longs to serve you,	
	whether some spell binds you	1330
	or if you are under some duress.	
	There is no Cyclops, no wizard,	
	no spell of Alcina,	
	no garden of Falerina,	
	no serpent nor monster	
	that can stop me.[12]	
	Let my strength prove to you	
	that I am as fierce as Gradasso,	
	as gallant as Ruggiero,	
	and as mad as Orlando.	1340
SANCHO	And I'm here to tell you	
	that with every step he takes	
	he's a match for that Great Asshole,	
	that Rude Gerald,	
	and even that Old Mango.[13]	
DON QUIXOTE	Didn't I just say that?	
	Who asked your opinion,	
	you ill-bred squire?	
LUCINDA	Clever squire.	
DOROTEA	Brilliant.	1350

---

12 *Alcina, Falerina*: sorceresses that impede the hero's progress. Alcina appears in Ariosto's *Orlando furioso*; Falerina in the "prequel," *Orlando innamorato*, by the Italian poet Boiardo.

13 Sancho is mangling the names of the heroes from Boiardo and Ariosto that Don Quixote has just mentioned.

FIDENO   You've cheered up, Lucinda.

LUCINDA   I needed the distraction.

DON QUIXOTE   (*To LUCINDA*) Won't you answer me?

LUCINDA   Can you shield me from
the blows of Fortune?

SANCHO   As long as Fortune doesn't come
wielding a club, he can.

DON QUIXOTE   What did you say?
Quiet!

SANCHO   That much and more can be done   1360
by my master, Don Quixote.
He is very firm, very strong.

DON QUIXOTE   At your service.

LUCINDA   God save you, sir knight.

FIDENO   Oh, this is delicious!

LUCINDA   Yet I cannot relish it.

DOROTEA   Are you tired of him?

LUCINDA   My sorrows weigh upon me.
Yet I would like to send him away
without offending him.   1370
(*To DON QUIXOTE*) Sir knight,
what worries me is that my ladies-in-waiting
are on the road as night falls,
in a coach just beyond that bend.

If you were to escort them...

DON QUIXOTE Will your grace command me to go?

LUCINDA   It would be a great favor.

DON QUIXOTE Well then off I go!
             Ready my steed, Sancho.

SANCHO   I left him tied to a tree around here somewhere.   1380

DON QUIXOTE Lace up my enchanted helmet.

FIDENO   What a brave knight-errant!

SANCHO gives the helmet to DON QUIXOTE and they both exit

LUCINDA   Oh, Dorotea!

DOROTEA   What is causing you such distress?

LUCINDA   Many evils and little hope of good.
            My father says I must marry,
            and cruelly wants me to accept
            the man he's chosen
            rather than the one I love.
            It's no wonder I am miserable!   1390
            I've spent my life waiting for my love,
            and now I'm being ushered to my death.

*Enter the MARQUÉS, in traveling clothes, and the SERVANT who
LUCINDA sent to fetch him*

SERVANT   I've brought you to the place she commanded.

MARQUÉS   What is this?

FIDENO   The Marqués, here?
          You are very welcome, my lord.

DOROTEA   (*Aside*) Why has he come?
          Oh, traitor, how can you do this to me?

LUCINDA   (*Aside*) Heaven, guide my words,
          for you see that I am right.   1400
          (*Aloud*) I wish to speak with your lordship.

MARQUÉS   I am at your service.

DOROTEA   (*Aside*) Oh Fortune,
          how your slings and arrows pierce me!
          I must resist my fate.

LUCINDA   Let's speak over here
          where we can be seen
          but not heard.

*The MARQUÉS and LUCINDA move apart from the others. DOROTEA
watches from afar*

DOROTEA   (*Aside*) This must be her champion,
          the lover and the beloved.   1410
          He will be chosen
          while the other man is scorned.
          And what of me?
          I am the unfortunate one,
          mocked and unhappy,
          begging him and telling him
          that I am afflicted, troubled...
          Oh, traitor!

LUCINDA   (*To MARQUÉS*) My lord, hear me:
          not only am I not your equal,   1420

| | I also happen to hate you,
           | and will say it to your face.

| MARQUÉS | You spurn me for a man so lowly
           | he should consider himself lucky
           | to be my servant.

| LUCINDA | You are noble.
           | Would you stoop so low
           | as to give your name
           | to so humble a woman?
           | Behold the tearful countenance   1430
           | of this unfortunate woman
           | who weeps for honor
           | rather than for love.

| MARQUÉS | Calm down, you've made yourself clear.
           | Douse your burning rage
           | and wipe your tender eyes.
           | Cardenio has already told me of your love,
           | and I have come here
           | to be his best man,
           | not your bridegroom.   1440
           | You must marry Cardenio,
           | whether or not your father approves.

| LUCINDA | I am at your feet.

| MARQUÉS | (*Aside*) She has fallen for my trick.

| DOROTEA | (*Aside*) She was just pleading with him
           | and now she's overwhelmed with gratitude.
           | My suspicions are confirmed—
           | there's no escaping my misfortune.

| LUCINDA | You have revived my hope

	with the kindness	1450
	you bestow upon me.	
	I will trust in you.	

MARQUÉS As well you may.

LUCINDA I must be on my way.
It's late and my father is waiting for me.

SERVANT Your carriage is ready.

MARQUÉS God be with you.

LUCINDA God keep you.

DOROTEA (*Aside*) Is this to be my fate?

MARQUÉS (*Aside*) Now I burn even more.   1460

DOROTEA (*To LUCINDA*) You seem happier now.

LUCINDA My sorrows are ended.

Exit LUCINDA, FIDENO, and SERVANT

DOROTEA (*Aside*) And you leave me in hell
now that I've seen the truth.
Heaven help me!

The MARQUÉS notices DOROTEA

MARQUÉS (*Aside*) I cannot listen to her complaints now.
I have my own jealousy to tend to.

DOROTEA (*Aside*) I am dead.

Marqués	(*Aside*) I can hardly stand the sight of this woman!
Dorotea	(*Aloud*) It's just the two of us now, 1470 you laughing and me crying. You've had your fun, though it has cost me my life. So laugh away while I do nothing but weep.
Marqués	(*Aside*) I must get away.
Dorotea	Are you leaving, you traitor?
Marqués	(*Aside*) It's impossible to argue with a woman, especially when she is right.
Dorotea	Stop.
Marqués	(*Aloud*) I promise I will hear you out, 1480 but not right now...
Dorotea	Stop, you ingrate!
Marqués	Think about where we are...
Dorotea	Now you're worried about decency...
Marqués	And your father...
Dorotea	...and respect! Oh, traitor!
Marqués	How dare you?
Dorotea	Have you no pity?
Marqués	What do you want from me? 1490

	Have you lost your mind?
Dorotea	Because of you.
Marqués	Have you no honor?
Dorotea	I entrusted it to you.
Marqués	Let go! How she carries on!
Dorotea	Are you running away from me? Face me!
Marqués	Just my luck.

The MARQUÉS exits

Dorotea	Oh villain, you drive me mad!	1500
	Oh traitor, I renounce you!	
	May you burn with the fire	
	that spews from my mouth!	
	May Heaven deny you all happiness,	
	all your hopes and ambitions!	
	May my curses trip you up	
	and drag you into my misery.	
	Do not deceive yourself,	
	oh cruel one, I will follow you	
	to the ends of the earth.	1510
	My revenge will poison	
	Lucinda's heart against you.	

Just as DOROTEA is about to follow the MARQUÉS, a SQUIRE, a MATRON, a MAID, and some of LUCINDA's servants enter with DON QUIXOTE, who stops DOROTEA

DON QUIXOTE	Where are you going? My lady, are you out of your mind?
DOROTEA	Is it that obvious?
DON QUIXOTE	Tell me your sorrows and leave them to me.
DOROTEA	Why do you detain me while I can still hear the footsteps of the one who is fleeing? 1520 That pretender, that thief, who, with coercion and guile, stole my most valuable treasure, and then pawned it elsewhere! Oh women, do not trust men who promise so much!

DOROTEA exits. DON QUIXOTE starts to go after her but is stopped by the MATRON

DON QUIXOTE	Death to the thief!
MATRON	Where are you going, Mr. Knight-Errant? How little you know about love! Is it not against the laws of chivalry 1530 to rush off into a new adventure while in the middle of another?
DON QUIXOTE	Well said, fair lady, forgive me. I have erred.
MATRON	Fair, you say? That's nice to hear.
DON QUIXOTE	Rest here, my ladies,

| | while those nags |
| | graze over there. |

| SQUIRE | We have a long way to go | 1540 |
| | before nightfall. |

MAID	How can I rest now?
	I am offended and jealous.
	To call another woman beautiful,
	right in front of me?
	I never!

SQUIRE	You mean instead of this young maid,
	you'll take that old maid over there?
	What nonsense.

DON QUIXOTE	An old woman's love is freer,	1550
	if not as frisky.
	Everyone knows that old Corisanda
	tended to the young knight Florestán.[14]

| MATRON | Someone will tend to you too. |

| SQUIRE | Between the sheets. |

| MAID | So you don't want me anymore? |

DON QUIXOTE	One who has defeated ten giants
	surely has the strength
	to love two women, at least.

SQUIRE	You'll need that strength and more.	1560
	It's easier to defeat a million giants
	than to love two women.

---

14   *Corisanda, Florestán*: in *Amadís de Gaula*, Corisanda keeps Florestán beholden to her in an amorous relationship, refusing to let him leave her side.

	You must be truly courageous if that's what you aim to do.
Don Quixote	At times like these I become Leander the Courageous.[15]
Maid	So you'll be my Leander?
Don Quixote	The one who swam across the Hellespont.
Maid	Don't you recognize me? I am your beloved Hero!
Don Quixote	You're Hero?
Maid	The one you swam to every night.
Squire	She's the one, for sure.
Maid	If you swim across the straits, you can breach my ramparts.
Matron	Are you up for it?
Don Quixote	I have courage and spirit enough for the widest strait.
Matron	The wider the strait, the easier the entry.
Don Quixote	I can ride the water like a ship with bulging sails.

---

15   *Leander*: In the Greek myth of Hero and Leander, Hero would leave a light shining in a tower window to guide her lover Leander as he swam across the Hellespont to her every night, until one night the light was blown out and Leander drowned.

SQUIRE   If you're going to swim,
                  you need to keep your clothes dry.
                  That way, if you drown
                  you only risk your hide.

DON QUIXOTE I'll be after you like a bullet.

MATRON   If you swim like a lead bullet,
                  you'll sink at once,
                  unless a dolphin comes to your rescue.   1590

DON QUIXOTE I'm sure to reach your tower,
                  as long as you leave a light on for me.

MAID   Don't you worry about that.
                  I have a candle…
                  and plenty of places to stick it.

DON QUIXOTE Let's rehearse what you will say
                  when I come into your arms,
                  all wet and undone.

MAID   If you come too soon,
                  you'll leave me cold.   1600
                  But I'll still say:
                  Oh, my sweet Leander!

DON QUIXOTE Oh, Hero of my soul!
                  And what else will you say?

MAID   My words are yet to come…

DON QUIXOTE How wet I'll be…

SQUIRE   A fine madman!

DON QUIXOTE	Oh beauteous Hero,
	let me take off my clothes right now
	so I can practice my swimming. 1610
MATRON	Just what we need!
MAID	Hold on, my Leander.
	No one but me
	should see your courage.
DON QUIXOTE	My love waits on your desire.
SQUIRE	Look at him now!
	Will he die like Leander
	or love like Lancelot?[16]

Enter SANCHO

SANCHO	Oh, my master, there you are!
DON QUIXOTE	Is that you, Sancho? 1620
SANCHO	I wish I weren't!
DON QUIXOTE	Now I will do great deeds.
	Was it a dragon or a giant
	that you ran into?
SANCHO	Rocinante chased some mares
	and their owners weren't amused.
	So they cracked his ribs with their staffs,
	curse them.
DON QUIXOTE	I beg your leave, my lady.

---

16   *Lancelot*: One of King Arthur's knights of the round table and a famous adulterer.

MAID	I grant it.	1630

DON QUIXOTE Halt, you heinous creatures,
you base knaves, here I come!

DON QUIXOTE charges off and SANCHO follows

SQUIRE He should bottle that courage and sell it.

MATRON His madness is incredible.

SQUIRE Let's get into the carriage
and leave him to it.
It's late, and we should
get to the house before dark.

MATRON Let's go. What an amusing madman.

SQUIRE	An extraordinary one.	1640

MAID My spirited Leander
has left me high and dry.

SCENE 3

Garden of a country estate

Enter LUCINDA at the window

LUCINDA Aid me, oh heavens, amid so much pain.
I can no more plot against their strength
than find the strength to resist their plot.
I know now that my father and the Marqués
have conspired against me.
One is cruel, the other a traitor.

	Even the servants,	
	though they pity me,	1650
	have been threatened into complicity.	
	This open window is my only chance.	
	Through it I will either find help	
	or, in despair, I will throw myself from it.	
	There is not a creature in sight,	
	much to my dismay.	
	But who would be out at this hour	
	except some tormented soul?	

Enter DOROTEA *cross-dressed as a country lad*

DOROTEA (*Aside*) In these clothes
I will put an end to my sorrows.   1660
Love lights a fire in me
and gives me the courage to seek revenge.
My enemy, the Marqués,
is in this house,
and though he robbed me of my life,
I am resolved to hound him
for the rest of his days.

LUCINDA   Where are you going, my young friend?

DOROTEA (*Aside*) You, calling me friend?
Woe is me, you are my enemy,   1670
through no fault of your own.
(*Aloud*) What is it, my lady?

LUCINDA   Come closer,
I need your help.
Listen, tell me:
do you know Cardenio?

DOROTEA   Doesn't he serve the Duke?

LUCINDA   I wish it weren't so.
          You must deliver a message for me without delay.
          May your every wish come true,   1680
          may you enjoy a thousand years of happiness—
          but no more, you must not delay.
          Take this chain as your reward—
          but wait, it's too heavy
          and will only slow you down.
          Take this diamond instead,
          it won't get in your way...

DOROTEA   But if—

LUCINDA   No ifs, no buts.
          You risk my hopes with any delay.   1690
          Hear me now: take this letter,
          half-written, unsealed,
          and place it in Cardenio's hands.
          Tell him they will marry me off
          to the Marqués tonight.
          If he does not rescue me,
          he will deliver me
          into the arms of another.

DOROTEA   Of course, of course!

LUCINDA   Go, go!   1700
          Tell him... I can't speak...
          that the Marqués...

DOROTEA   Don't trouble yourself.
          No need for more explanations,
          I understand.

LUCINDA   Tell him that my father and the Marqués
          have conspired to betray me.

              The Marqués, with his trickery,
              has brought me to this remote house,
              to this tower surrounded by fields,   1710
              at the foot of these wild mountains.
              And tell him, if he comes quickly,
              there is a door I could leave open
              and then his courage could finally...

DOROTEA   Of course, of course.

LUCINDA   Go, go—
              Wait, what am I saying?
              I've forgotten the most important part.

DOROTEA   Don't trouble yourself,
              just finish your thought,   1720
              or your delays will be the end of us.

LUCINDA   Tell him that I will set a light
              at the top of this tower,
              so that if he comes at night
              it can be his North Star,
              and if he sees the lantern burning,
              he may come to my rescue.
              But tell him that if the light is no more,
              then neither am I, and he must forgive me.

                  LUCINDA picks up a knife

              With this blade, I will end my life.   1730
              Tell him to think well of me,
              and not to grieve for me,
              and to save himself.

DOROTEA   Of course, of course.

LUCINDA   Go, go...
               Wait, don't go,
               tell him that...
               Oh, this will be the end of me!

DOROTEA   Don't trouble yourself,
               but do get to the point.   1740
               You'll drown us both in your tears.

LUCINDA   Tell him to forget what he owes the Marqués
               and think of what he owes to me.
               Tell him not to concern himself
               with the trappings of marriage.
               If no one will help us,
               we will live in a cave
               in the heart of the mountains.
               I will be happier there with him
               than as a great lady.   1750

DOROTEA   Of course, of course.

LUCINDA   Go, go...
               I am so afraid...
               Oh my love...

DOROTEA   Please stop.
               (*Aside*) I can't believe this woman.
               I'm this close to telling her who I am.

LUCINDA   I'm in such a state.
               Am I making sense?
               Are you clear on what you must say?   1760
               Repeat it back to me.
               You will forget something important
               and ruin everything if you are careless.

DOROTEA   (*Aloud*) Have no fear, your words will stay with me.
             You have given me winged feet
             and quickened my heart like mercury.¹⁷
             This fire in my chest
             will make me as fast as lightning.

LUCINDA   Just one more thing—

DOROTEA   I can't take it anymore!   1770

LUCINDA   Then go.

DOROTEA   I fly.

LUCINDA   Go, go.

Exit LUCINDA *and* DOROTEA

SCENE 4

Outside a country estate

Enter DON QUIXOTE *and* SANCHO PANZA

SANCHO   Where's your trusty Rocinante?

DON QUIXOTE Poor battered creature,
             beaten by such a scoundrel.
             Had I caught him,
             I would have shown him
             that he was born under an unlucky star.

SANCHO   Well, since he got away,   1780

---

17 *Mercury*: Also known as quicksilver, this liquid metal was used as a catalyst for chemical reactions in alchemy.

it must not have been so unlucky.
That's how it goes!
Who would believe that Rocinante
would suffer such a fate
when he is such a peaceful horse?

DON QUIXOTE   Even so...
He is lightning itself in battle,
worth his weight in gold,
brilliant as Orlando's Brilladoro[18]
and the great Babieca of El Cid.   1790

SANCHO   He's an exemplary horse,
the best of his kind.
He can go four days without food
and not say a word.

DON QUIXOTE   Horses can't talk, you fool!

SANCHO   Can too! And in verse, no less.
Haven't you heard the ballad that goes:
"*There he is, there he is,
You must kill him where he stands!*"[19]
Babieca spoke in that one.   1800

DON QUIXOTE   Well said, by God!
And then it goes:
"*Even Mary was not as surprised
when her baby burst forth.*"
Since you've figured this out,
good Sancho, maybe from now on

---

18   *Brilladoro, Babieca*: These references to famous horses from epic and chivalric romance in turn reference an episode from the novel where Quixote's horse Rocinante finds himself in trouble after getting frisky with some mares.

19   A reference at least partially from the ballad of "The Moorish King Who Lost Valencia," though these lines do not appear in their entirety in that poem.

| | you can be in charge
                  of asking Rocinante his opinion. |

| SANCHO | He might tell us,
           but from what I hear   1810
           Rocinante is a little hoarse. |

| DON QUIXOTE | How dark it's gotten!
                Hero has not lit the lantern.
                Has she fallen asleep? |

| SANCHO | I don't know what you're talking about. |

| DON QUIXOTE | I am Leander. |

| SANCHO | Will this transformation
           require another beating
           like when you became Valdovinos? |

| DON QUIXOTE | Quiet. Oh Hero, herald of love!   1820 |

| SANCHO | I hope those giants don't come back
           for a second helping. |

| DON QUIXOTE | Don't be silly.
                If they do,
                it will be to my greater glory. |

| SANCHO | What are you talking about now? |

| DON QUIXOTE | I'm on the shore of the Hellespont.
                Can't you see how the sea roars?
                Can't you hear the poor ships
                being tossed by the storm?   1830 |

| SANCHO | The only thing I hear is

DON QUIXOTE the frogs croaking in the pond.

DON QUIXOTE Great things can never be grasped by the lowly,
who only perceive things as they are.

SANCHO What's this? What do you mean?
Can't you feel the ground beneath your feet?
Don't you see the mountains over there?
How can you deny it?
Where is this shore, where is this sea?

DON QUIXOTE Can't you see the light in that tower there? 1840
What do you say to that?
Isn't that proof enough?

DON QUIXOTE starts undressing

SANCHO I'm going crazy.
Now you're taking your clothes off?
Hold on!

DON QUIXOTE I want to cross the strait.
I will swim like a fish
to reach my bliss.
Oh, tower of Hero!
Oh, light of my life! 1850
Undress me.

SANCHO But where's the water?

DON QUIXOTE How can you ask me that?
Have you lost your senses?

SANCHO If you dive onto dry land,
you're gonna break your nose.

DON QUIXOTE   Don't you know how to swim?

SANCHO   Yeah, when there's water!

DON QUIXOTE   Oh, tower of Hero!
Oh, light of my life!   1860
Undress me.

SANCHO   What are you doing?

DON QUIXOTE   I will swim to my Hero.

DON QUIXOTE continues to take off his clothes

SANCHO   I don't believe this!
Are you dreaming?
Aren't we standing on solid ground?

DON QUIXOTE   Leave me be.

SANCHO   What do you mean 'leave me be'?
You're going to kill yourself, watch out!

DON QUIXOTE begins swimming on the stage, as if he were in the water

DON QUIXOTE   What may be land to you   1870
is the rolling sea to me.
Watch me float like a feather.

SANCHO   You're going to fall flat on your face![20]

DON QUIXOTE   See how I break through the waves.

SANCHO   As long as you don't break wind.

---

20   Perhaps a metatheatrical suggestion that he's about to fall off the stage.

Look out, or you'll break your bones.

DON QUIXOTE Where did the light go?
I must be blind.
Beautiful Hero, I'm almost there,
open your arms to me.

DON QUIXOTE exits, swimming, then CARDENIO and DOROTEA enter

SANCHO Is someone there? I'll hide myself.

SANCHO hides

DOROTEA (*To CARDENIO*) You've ridden that horse into the ground.

SANCHO (*Aside*) Oh, why the devil did I decide
to become a knight-errant?

DOROTEA We've arrived.

CARDENIO At the place of my death.
The light is out now.

DOROTEA (*Aside*) Just my luck.
(*Aloud*) Perhaps they're trimming the wick
to make it shine brighter.

CARDENIO Or perhaps the wind has blown it out?
(*Aside*) But what wind?
I'm out of my mind.
Oh harsh fortune!

DOROTEA That would be the cruelest wind to ever blow.

CARDENIO A minute's delay has been my undoing.

| | Oh gentle heavens,
have you no mercy on me? |
|---|---|
| DOROTEA | (*Aside*) And what of me?
(*Aloud*) Wait, wait! 1900 |
| CARDENIO | Can you see the light? |
| DOROTEA | No, not now.
It must've been lightning. |
| CARDENIO | I wish it would strike my heart,
for my happiness is as fleeting
as a flash of lightning! |
| DOROTEA | Aren't these the tower walls?
Do I hear someone calling? |
| CARDENIO | You're right, let's get closer. |
| DOROTEA | You first. 1910 |

Enter the MATRON

MATRON	Cardenio, is that you?
CARDENIO	The unlucky one!
MATRON	It's no one's fault but your own.
What took you so long?
CARDENIO	I came as fast as I could.
MATRON	My lady waited here for you
until her father became so angry
that he almost dragged her off

>   by the hair to marry the Marqués.
>
> DOROTEA   Oh unyielding Fortune!   1920
>
> CARDENIO   This is the end of me!
>   Oh, my love!
>
> MATRON   Come in, that was her request.
>
> CARDENIO   What's this, do the heavens now smile upon me?
>
> MATRON   Bring the messenger along with you—
>   that way we'll have another witness.
>   Hurry!
>
> DOROTEA   Oh, the ways of men!
>
> CARDENIO   Oh, the ways of women!
>
> MATRON   Come in, my friend,   1930
>   you can trust me.
>
> DOROTEA   And I'm here beside you
>   to help you seize your chance.
>
> *Exit all*

SCENE 5

A room in a country estate

Enter the MARQUÉS, TEODORO, and SERVANTS

> TEODORO   Forgive her childish nonsense, Marqués.
>   Lucinda is still young.

>   Soon your love will conquer her modesty.
>   It won't take long.
>   (*To the* SERVANTS) Tell Lucinda to come out,
>   for the Marqués is here.
>
>   *Enter* LUCINDA, *the* MATRON, *and the* MAID
>
>   Here she comes now.   1940

MARQUÉS   There she is, lovely as the dawn,
                yet still a bit upset.
                How can a woman be so stubborn?

LUCINDA   (*Aside*) Can this be called marriage
                if my will is forced?
                Since my enemies will have it thus,
                may my name join the ranks
                of the Portias and Lucretias,
                who took their lives for their honor.[21]

Enter CARDENIO *through one door and* DOROTEA *through another,*
unseen by the others

CARDENIO   (*Aside*) Oh queen of beauty!   1950

DOROTEA   (*Aside*) Oh unfortunate woman!
                Now I must witness my own death.

CARDENIO   (*Aside*) Is this honor?
                Is this fidelity?
                Must I be witness to this?

DOROTEA   (*Aside*) Has it come to this, you traitor?

---

21   *Portia, Lucretia*: Roman models of female virtue who committed suicide to demonstrate their devotion to their husbands or preserve their honor.

TEODORO	(*To LUCINDA*) Give him your hand.
LUCINDA	My lord…
CARDENIO	(*Aside*) Does she waver?
DOROTEA	(*Aside*) Does she tremble? 1960
CARDENIO	(*Aside*) Oh, kind heavens! Will she remember the love she owes me? Will she say no?
DOROTEA	(*Aside*) Oh God, she can't say no! Is there another way out?
TEODORO	(*To LUCINDA*) Why do you hesitate?
LUCINDA	Marqués, I…
MARQUÉS	Her heart is as hard as a diamond.
CARDENIO	(*Aside*) Stand firm!
DOROTEA	(*Aside*) Say no! 1970
TEODORO	Give him your hand or else!
LUCINDA	Oh unlucky me! Heaven be my witness that I do this against my will!
CARDENIO	(*Aside*) You have killed me, Lucinda!

Exit CARDENIO

DOROTEA	(*Aside*) You have ruined me, Marqués!
MARQUÉS	What voices were those? Was that Cardenio?
LUCINDA	Oh God!

LUCINDA faints

TEODORO	Heavens above! Have you ever seen such a thing? Here's a note in her bodice, and a dagger up her sleeve!
MARQUÉS	What are you saying?

LUCINDA awakens

LUCINDA	I was not brave enough. I should have killed myself when I had the chance, but now it's too late.
TEODORO	Oh the shame of it all! She is the source of all my misfortune!
MARQUÉS	How insulting! This is beyond disdain. I will kill her for this.
TEODORO	Don't be so rash. All is not lost—
LUCINDA	Go on then, kill me. All I want from you is death!

Marqués	May the heavens smite you!
Lucinda	I'll gladly become a martyr. 2000
Marqués	Then I'll kill your soulmate instead, for Cardenio is not immortal. I will take my revenge on that peasant. I'll cut out that tongue I just heard cry out.
Teodoro	Have some pity for these gray hairs, and think of my misfortune.
Marqués	I'll find him even if I have to tear this house apart!
Teodoro	Wait, my lord, you are blinded by rage!
Marqués	The flame of my rage will burn this place to the ground! 2010
Teodoro	Please remember this is my house and it deserves respect.
Marqués	Yet it harbors a traitor.
Teodoro	None of my blood.
Marqués	Where are my men?
Teodoro	My servants, come to my aid!
Lucinda	What madness!
Teodoro	Come, loyal servants!

Exit Teodoro and Marqués. Dorotea reveals herself to Lucinda

DOROTEA   (*To LUCINDA*) Now we'll both die of fright.

LUCINDA   Only God can save me now.　　　　　　2020

DOROTEA   Run, my lady.

LUCINDA   I must find my resolve.
           A wronged woman must save herself!

Exit all

End of Act II

ACT III

SCENE 1

A room in the DUKE's palace

Enter the DUKE and FULGENCIO, his servant

FULGENCIO	You would not believe the state the house was in.
DUKE	The very thought of it is horrible, but say more.
FULGENCIO	A thousand swords slashed through the air. Amid the wounded men, the ladies cried out, 2030 all in disarray, fainting at the sight. Some tried to burn the house down, while others defended it. This went on until the Marqués was convinced that Cardenio had come and gone through some secret door left ajar, and decided to chase after him. Some followed on horseback, and I on foot, 2040 though I could not keep up

| | with only these two poor feet.
But as I heard after,
they must have left Cardenio for dead
on some remote mountain,
since he hasn't turned up. |
| --- | --- |
| DUKE | Oh unlucky Cardenio!
I am a sad, cursed old man!
Oh, my terrible son!
Is this how you display our noble blood?   2050
How can the Marqués behave like this
and yet be mine?
He cannot be...
yet his mother, an angel,
gave birth to him...
so I must believe I am his father.
He must be punishment for my sins.
I've wondered a thousand times
if he was switched at birth,
though it's a terrifying thought.   2060
Who would do something so malicious?
How can I speak this aloud? Oh heavens!
What is it, Fulgencio? |
| FULGENCIO | I'm speechless, my lord!
I fear you may be getting carried away. |
| DUKE | It's not that far-fetched.
I spent my younger years
in love with an angel of a woman
who was everything to me.
She was less wealthy, but still noble.   2070
Yet my father, a man of the highest nobility,
insisted I marry one of my own rank.
Still, I loved her so much
that I made her my wife in secret. |

A year later my father found out
and quickly turned my joy to pain:
pleasure is fleeting and the truth will out.
I had to leave her in a convent,
where she gave birth to our son,
born under an unlucky star. 2080
A priest gave him
to the wife of the peasant Lisardo
so she could raise the babe
along with their son Cardenio,
who had just been born.
And so it was for twelve years
due to my father's stubborn anger,
until Heaven finally took him.
At last, after so long apart,
I brought my wife home. 2090
Then Lisardo brought me
the young Cardenio and the Marqués.
One is truly valiant,
the other is truly vile.
I love Cardenio
and loathe the Marqués.
In this unhappiness,
I have found ample reason
to doubt as I do.

Teodoro enters and kneels to the Duke

TEODORO   Forgive the intrusion, my lord, 2100
though I come not to beg forgiveness,
for who could blame a man
who transgresses only
to protect his honor?
My lord, I must ask you for redress
as an afflicted and affronted father,
deprived of his honor and his daughter...

	But surely you've already heard the rest.
DUKE	Rise.
TEODORO	This is my place. 2110
DUKE	No, it's not.
TEODORO	This note from Lucinda will tell you everything you need to know:

Hands the DUKE a note[22]

"Cardenio is my true husband. If I were to ever give my hand in marriage to the Marqués, it would be under paternal duress. I hid this knife so that with my death I could deprive the Marqués of the pleasure of thinking I am his. Behold my fidelity and weep. Lucinda."

TEODORO	When Lucinda fainted and we found this note, the Marqués... 2120
DUKE	May God smite him!
TEODORO	...took her from my house and brought her to yours.
DUKE	I burn with rage!
FULGENCIO	That cannot be, you've been misled. We have not seen the Marqués here.

---

22 Staging options open. Either man could read it aloud, or off-stage Lucinda could do a dramatic voiceover.

DUKE   Your honor is safe with me.
                Now I understand the situation,   2130
                so rest assured.

TEODORO   I kiss your feet a thousand times over.

                TEODORO rises and exits

DUKE   Though he be my son,
                I will renounce him.

                FIDENO enters and kneels to the DUKE

FIDENO   My lord, the Marqués has taken my daughter.
                Dorotea is missing from my house
                and she herself told me of his amorous intentions,
                so I must surmise it is he who has taken her.
                All I ask for is justice.
                See how I suffer, my lord,   2140
                for she was the light of my life
                and my very soul.

DUKE   Oh, villainous Marqués!
                What has he become?
                He'll pay for this in blood!
                Go, Fideno, and be satisfied,
                for I will not leave a drop of blood
                within his chest.

FIDENO   May you live a thousand years!

                Exit FIDENO, then enter LUCINDA, who prostrates herself before
                the DUKE

LUCINDA   My lord, I throw myself at your feet.   2150

DUKE	What's all this?
	Get up... Is this a dream...?
	Calm down... Is this some trick...?
LUCINDA	I am Cardenio's wife, my lord.
	Yet your son insists
	I must be his instead.
DUKE	How did you get away from him?
LUCINDA	With the help of heaven.
	Amid the confusion in my house,
	I dragged myself, half-dead, 2160
	and as I stumbled outside,
	I found a horse by the gate.
	An angel must have been watching over me,
	for the horse kept still while I mounted
	then flew off as my fear spurred it on
	while I wept so hard
	I could barely see the ground.
	My mind was shrouded in sorrow
	as dark as the night.
	I rode until dawn, 2170
	until I reached the house of a friend.
	She lent me this cloak
	and then I rushed here to ask you,
	in the name of heaven, to protect me.
	My lord, grant me this, as you are noble.
	As the wife of one
	who has served you well,
	I throw myself at your feet,
	seeking protection at your hands
	from those of the Marqués. 2180
DUKE	Rise.

LUCINDA   My suffering is too great.

DUKE   Take comfort and cry no more.
             I will protect you.

LUCINDA   Allow me—

DUKE   By holy heaven above,
             to avenge you as a woman
             and as the wife of one
             so dear to my heart,
             I will kill this villain!   2190

LUCINDA   Allow me to kiss your feet.

DUKE   Oh Marqués,
             my curses will hound you
             until I bring you down.

                        Exit all

SCENE 2

           A clearing in the mountains

Enter DON QUIXOTE *and* SANCHO *with a sack containing* DOROTEA's *clothing and* CARDENIO's *sword, cloak, and hat*

DON QUIXOTE Are you still complaining
             about the poor wages of knight-errantry?

SANCHO   Thank God today has paid off,
             after the mule drivers
             beat me with their clubs
             and the herdsmen hit me with their staffs.   2200

DON QUIXOTE	These are the wages of chivalry.
	He who rushes into such battles
	proves his steel and his valor.
	The greater the injuries,
	the braver the knight.
	Out of the ashes of war,
	he may emerge emperor of all.
	Quick, let's ride on,
	for this hat is made of good felt,
	and there's a sword and a cloak 2210
	and a jerkin and a whole world of things
	in that sack we found.
SANCHO	Oh boy, my luck has finally changed.
DON QUIXOTE	Are you happy at last?
SANCHO	This paunch of mine is bursting with joy,
	or my name isn't Sancho Panza.[23]
DON QUIXOTE	What shalt thou do, good Panza,
	when I finally conquer a fair isle for thee?
	You'll be a new Gandalín!
SANCHO	Ganda-who? 2220
DON QUIXOTE	He was the squire of Amadís,
	that marvel of marvels,
	who made him the lord
	of some fifty towns—
	as thou shalt be,
	though it cost me my life.
SANCHO	Just give me some vassals.

---

23 Panza means "belly" so he's punning on his name.

>   I'll know how to play the master,
>   make no mistake.

Don Quixote sniffs the sack

Don Quixote   What a sweet smell! 2230
    It is the finest perfume.
    This must belong to some nobleman,
    perhaps from the house of Amadís himself.
    What I'd give to know who this belongs to!

Sancho   May we never meet the owner.

Enter a Peasant

Don Quixote   Good man, I need your assistance!

Peasant   With what?

Sancho   But the owner isn't even looking for it!

Don Quixote   Hush.

Sancho   Rats! Can he not see 2240
    that finders should be keepers?

Don Quixote   Have you seen a knight at his wits' end
    who might have left these things behind?

Peasant   Yes, I have.

Sancho   I was hoping for a no.

Don Quixote   Get away from those things, Sancho.

Sancho   But they're mine now!

| PEASANT | I saw a man wandering around
| | like a loon some days back.
| | He was raging about, 2250
| | with no sense or reason.
| | Mad now, then sane,
| | but always noble in his demeanor.
| | He's never in one place for long,
| | but often comes here
| | and steals food from my boys,
| | scaring them out of their wits.
| | Other times he's in a softer mood
| | and begs for food instead.
| | Then he screams and wails, 2260
| | and throws himself about,
| | but doesn't speak a word.
| | His fits last over an hour.
| | When he does speak,
| | it's always the same tune:
| | "Lucinda has killed me,
| | the Marqués has betrayed me!"
| | Oh, there he is now!
| | Just look at his face.

DON QUIXOTE I'd give anything to know more about him. 2270

Enter CARDENIO, *wearing nothing but underclothes*

CARDENIO What rage burns in me, what fire!

PEASANT Just listen to him.

CARDENIO Has any man suffered like this?
Where will I find peace?
Where do my feet carry me,
lifeless as I am?
Oh, I'm losing my mind!

> But how could I stay sane
> when the Marqués has betrayed me?
> What reason could I muster 2280
> with no self, no soul, no you?
> Oh Lucinda, you have killed me!
> It's true what they say:
> death never comes to those who long for it.
> Will you not face me, Death,
> you cowardly villain?
> Come pay your debts,
> you who take so much from so many.
> Are you afraid of a poor wretch?
> Do you fear me, 2290
> weak as I am?
> Go against your nature, for once,
> and be kind to me!
> But how could you be kind
> if Lucinda can't be faithful?
> Oh Heaven above,
> if you will not smite me,
> or send some beast to devour me,
> or a bolt of lightning to strike me,
> will you not at least console me, 2300
> in such dire straits?
> Let the angels peer from the clouds
> and pour down comfort upon me.
> Will I ever see the sun and stars
> shine upon me again?
> But no, for I'll see Lucinda
> among them in the sky
> and only be reminded
> that the Marqués has enjoyed her.
> Oh, Lucinda has killed me, 2310
> the Marqués has betrayed me!

DON QUIXOTE What a fine line to end on!

PEASANT	It's all fun and games now,
	but just wait an hour.
DON QUIXOTE	I must know what's troubling him.
	Oh hello sir...
PEASANT	When he is in this state,
	he can't hear or see anything.
DON QUIXOTE	Oh sir, the most afflicted knight
	of all time was Amadís. 2320
	Do you hear me, sir?
	Are you listening?
SANCHO	You'll have to speak up.
DON QUIXOTE	Come back!
	You'll like what I have to say,
	I assure you.
SANCHO	You have to speak louder.
	You there, my friend!
CARDENIO	What do you want from me?
	Your poor manners 2330
	have me at my wits' end.
	Let me go back to my dreams,
	sleepless though I may be.
	I was dreaming I was a diamond
	wrapped around Lucinda's finger,
	once again in her favor,
	pressed against her skin.
	And now in my mind's eye
	she's back in the arms of the Marqués.
	Take this, you fools, 2340
	for robbing me of that glorious vision.

Cardenio begins to punch and kick them

Don Quixote Stop it, you madman!

Cardenio Traitors!

Sancho Ow!

Peasant Ow!

Cardenio I'll kill you!

Don Quixote *Crimes caused by love*
should be pardoned all above.[24]

Cardenio I'll take my wounded heart
and return to my treasured solitude.

Exit Cardenio

Sancho My poor back—it's broken.

Peasant I am dead.

Don Quixote I am wounded.

Peasant Scoundrel!

Sancho What a gentleman!
(*To* **Peasant**) You donkey's ass,
you could've warned us
this guy was dangerous.
I oughta—

---

24 A proverbial phrase that finds its origin in the ballad of *Conde Claros of Montalván* (16th century): "Yerros de amor son dignos de perdonar."

PEASANT	I did warn you, you drunk!	2360
SANCHO	You're calling me a drunk? You seem like you've had a few yourself.	
PEASANT	Are you calling me a liar? You'd better watch yourself.	
SANCHO	Oh, I'm watching.	

SANCHO and PEASANT fight

DON QUIXOTE	Enough! Stop this! Get off each other! A knight tells you to stop and you keep going? You scoundrels, you rascals, you scalawags!	2370
SANCHO	Your quests always end in a brawl, sir.	
PEASANT	By God! You are every bit as crazy as that madman who just ran off.	
DON QUIXOTE	Get up, Sancho, let's go!	
SANCHO	I can't.	
PEASANT	May God keep you down forever!	

Exit PEASANT

SANCHO	That went well.	
DON QUIXOTE	In any case, I have no doubt the madman must be a great knight. Such a devoted lover,	2380

so fierce, so gallant, so brave.
I am envious of how well
he imitated the famous Orlando
in his jealous madness.

SANCHO He was a little too mad for me.
He seemed more like Beelzebub.

DON QUIXOTE What do you know of chivalry, you beast?
Orlando's all-consuming jealousy
when his Angelica ran off with Medoro[25]
made him bellow like a bull. 2390

SANCHO Did he have horns like a bull too?[26]

DON QUIXOTE He peeled off his armor, sword, and shield
until he was as naked as the day he was born.
He knocked the daylights out of many men,
and rode his horse into the ground.
All this he did in his famous madness.
The madness of Amadís
was more human in its scope.
Scorned by Oriana,
he chose to do penance at the Peña Pobre. 2400
He changed his name to Beltenebros,[27]
wept, withdrew from the world,
and thereby made a name for himself.
What must I do for my feats
to become as famous?
Is my lady not as beautiful?

---

25 *Orlando, Medoro, Angelica*: In *Orlando furioso*, Angelica chooses Medoro and drives Orlando mad with jealous sorrow, in a parallel to Cardenio's fear that Lucinda has chosen the Marqués.

26 Horns were associated with being cuckolded.

27 *Beltenebros*: The Prince of Shadows, in *Amadís*. This episode introduces a darker tone, echoed in Cardenio's madness and mocked in Quixote's imitation.

| | Am I not as valiant? |
| | Am I missing something? |

Sancho   If you must know,
              I will tell you the truth: 2410
              even in these nonsense tales
              of madness and hot air,
              those knights had a reason to be jealous.
              Who has made you jealous
              or given you the cold shoulder?
              Who has stomped on your heart?
              Does your lady love a Medoro,
              or some other knight, or a squire?
              Has she been trifling with you?
              I don't see what you have to complain about, sir. 2420

Don Quixote   This is all so I can show Dulcinea
              just how much I love her.
              Even without a good reason,
              I can still reach the depths of despair.
              If this is how I carry on
              when the weather is fair,
              imagine me in a storm!
              I know what I must do now.

Sancho   What now, my lord?

Don Quixote   I am mad, I must be mad,   2430
              I won't hear otherwise.
              Oh Death, why do you not take me?
              Have my misfortunes scared you away?
              In this, I'll be one part Orlando
              and one part Amadís.

Sancho   There's a recipe for success.

DON QUIXOTE   Let me finish.
              Off with you, breastplate and gauntlets!
              My sword, I renounce you!
              Farewell, shield of Orlando!   2440
              Goodbye, helm of Mambrino!²⁸
              Sancho, go hang these up from that tree there.
              Then you will be following in the footsteps
              of Cervín, the famed squire of Orlando.

SANCHO   The next thing to go
              will be your wits, and then mine.

DON QUIXOTE   Oh Heavens,
              will you not grant me death
              among the beasts of these mountains
              and the satyrs of these woods?   2450
              Oh angels on high,
              look down upon me
              and vomit up some heavenly balm²⁹
              to purge the venom from my soul.
              Where are my feet carrying me?
              How can I keep myself together
              when Dulcinea is tearing me apart?

SANCHO   And don't forget to say:
              "The Marqués has tricked me."
              That's what the other guy said.   2460

DON QUIXOTE   I am betwixt and between,
              sleeping as I wake,
              all for my beautiful enemy, Dulcinea!

---

28   *Helm of Mambrino*: Quixote's famous helmet, ostensibly a prized piece of armor from *Orlando furioso*, but actually a shaving basin.

29   *Balm*: In the Spanish, "triaca"—a fabled panacea for all poisons, searched for by alchemists. This moment echoes the language of Cardenio when he's shouting to the heavens, now in a much sillier version.

| SANCHO | He's really trying
to imitate him in every way.
It's getting late, sir! | |
|---|---|---|
| DON QUIXOTE | Hush now, peasant.
I was dreaming that Dulcinea
was holding me in her arms
and you ruined it.
For that, I should kill you! | 2470 |

DON QUIXOTE hits SANCHO

SANCHO	Hey, hey!
DON QUIXOTE	Don't I make a good madman?
SANCHO	Yes, sir, unluckily for me.
Do you really have to imitate
all his kicks and punches?
DON QUIXOTE	I will stay my hand just to say...
SANCHO	What now?

| DON QUIXOTE | ...that you must bring my lady
a letter on my behalf.
Among the shrubbery,
I will find a gloomy cave
and howl for my misfortunes
like Beltenebros himself. | 2480 |
|---|---|---|
| SANCHO | Should I go now? | |
| DON QUIXOTE | Yes, and when you return,
you'll find me both mournful and merry.
Come see where I'll stay | |

                    and I'll tell you what to do.
                    But first you must witness   2490
                    how I descend into madness
                    so you can relay it all to Dulcinea.
                    I will run headlong into those rocks
                    over and over.

SANCHO   And I will take her
                    your broken skull as proof.

                    Exit DON QUIXOTE and SANCHO

                    ## SCENE 3

                    In the mountains

                    Enter CARDENIO, the PRIEST, and the BARBER

PRIEST   Your misfortune has moved me.

BARBER   And me.

CARDENIO   And you have both consoled me.
                    The heavens must have guided you here.   2500

PRIEST   May the same heavens
                    give you patience and respite.

CARDENIO   Forgive me, you must be tired of my woes.

BARBER   No, no, continue,
                    if it comforts you.

PRIEST   One who shares his sorrow
                    lessens his grief.

CARDENIO   I couldn't believe how poorly I was treated
           by those two—a man so high-born
           and an angel of a woman.   2510
           She summoned me there
           just so I could see her marry another.
           I thought she wanted
           to show me her fidelity.
           I was certain I would hear
           a "no" from her lips.
           I was sure she'd hesitate
           to give him her hand.
           I was waiting to hear her bravely say:
           "I cannot give you my hand, my lord."   2520
           I heard instead: "It is yours."
           I was left heartbroken, frozen,
           but with a fire raging in my chest.
           I fled as fast as lightning.
           My senses lost, I ran to the woods,
           disturbing their calm
           with a thousand screams and howls.
           And though I longed
           to fall on my own sword,
           it was nowhere to be found,   2530
           for I had flung it away.
           It must have been a miracle.
           The heavens took my senses
           so I would not take my life.
           I know that I suffer frequent fits of madness.
           My only hint of sanity
           is the knowledge that I am mad.

PRIEST   Calm yourself.
           You must look to God for consolation.

           Enter SANCHO with a sack of clothes

Barber	Is that Panza?	2540
Priest	Yes, to be sure. Sancho?	
Sancho	The Priest and the Barber!	
Barber	What's new, my friend?	
Sancho	What isn't new, compadre?	
Barber	Give me a hug!	
Sancho	(*Sees* CARDENIO) Oh no, it's him! By God, I better run.	
Barber	What are you running from? Wait!	2550
Sancho	From that man there! I'm still black and blue from the last time we met.	
Priest	He will do you no harm.	
Sancho	All right, I'll stay, if you're sure.	
Cardenio	It must have been one of my fits. That happens from time to time.	
Priest	Where is your master?	
Sancho	He's back there, in his own world, doing penance for a sin he never committed.	2560

PRIEST	What do you mean?
SANCHO	He's wearing as little as possible, unarmed and unclothed, living in a cave. He lies on the cold earth, imitating some gloomy Gus who stayed in the dark 2570 even in the middle of the day.
PRIEST	You mean Beltenebros?[30]
SANCHO	Yeah, him.
BARBER	What a crackpot.
PRIEST	I have never heard such a tale. But now where are you going?
SANCHO	I'm off to take a letter from my master to Dulcinea and her answer better be good, or he'll never leave that cave. 2580 Unless, of course, some great princess sends him on a big adventure. That's what he swore to do, and so he'll have to.
PRIEST	How peculiar. Ah, poor Mister Quijada! We must come up with a plan to get him out of there.
BARBER	Yes, let's think of something.

---

30   Even the Priest reads the chivalric romances closely enough to remember details.

	What's that you have there?	2590
Sancho	Oh, just this and that.	
Priest	Let's see what you have.	
Sancho	No way! A certain someone might see them and want them back.	
Cardenio	I think I recognize them, but don't worry about it.	
Sancho	If they are yours, can I have them?	
Cardenio	Yes, you may.	2600
Sancho	Did you hear that? He promised.	
Cardenio	And I'll vow a thousand times over.	
Sancho	These are some nice clothes.	
Cardenio	Tokens from a better time, abandoned by a mind unsound.	
Sancho	*And by me, mostly happily found.*[31]	
Priest	Very poetic.	
Barber	Bravo.	

---

31 Line referencing Garcilaso de la Vega's Sonnet X: "Oh dulces prendas por mi mal halladas"

SANCHO	I found them in an enchanted wood.	2610
PRIEST	As well a squire should.	
SANCHO	And they will do me good.	
BARBER	I hear footsteps.	
SANCHO	People are coming. I have to hide my prize.	
CARDENIO	There's a spring behind that rock. Someone must be headed for it.	

Enter DOROTEA, still disguised as a shepherd boy

DOROTEA	I am so tired, and still lost. When will my unlucky stars put an end to this sad life of mine? Where will all my misfortunes lead? And now the blazing sun compounds the fire in my breast.	2620
BARBER	Sounds like a woman's voice.	
CARDENIO	And one I've heard before.	
PRIEST	Let's go this way, quietly, so we can see what she does.	
SANCHO	That's not a woman; that's a boy!	
PRIEST	Hush, Sancho.	
SANCHO	I hush.	2630
BARBER	Shhhh.	

DOROTEA Is this a spring at last?
I come in search of its crystal waters
like a wounded doe.
Oh how gladly I would drink
if only these waters could quench
the fire in my heart.
But alas, I know this fire
will not be quenched with water,
since all the tears I've cried   2640
have only stoked it all the more.
Oh fierce heat, I'm dying!
Everything afflicts and torments me!
Even my hair is driving me mad.
Not even a comb could save it now.

DOROTEA takes off her hat, letting down her hair

BARBER She's certainly lovely.

PRIEST And much afflicted.

SANCHO Oh what my master wouldn't give
to see such a great adventure!

CARDENIO Women, too, can suffer as I do.   2650
Let's get closer.

PRIEST All right.

CARDENIO My lady?

DOROTEA Who are you?

CARDENIO The sight of your suffering
compels us to—

DOROTEA Oh no!

Dorotea starts to leave

BARBER
Is that how you answer us?
My lady, wait.
We're here to help you.
What do you say to that?

DOROTEA
What else am I supposed to do?
You've seen through my disguise...

CARDENIO
Calm down.
Can't you see we're here to help you?
We don't want to upset you.

DOROTEA
I believe you.
Your courteous manner
reveals your good intentions.

CARDENIO
(*Aside*) I know this voice,
but I have never seen this woman before.

DOROTEA
(*Aside*) Could that be Cardenio?
I recognize his voice.
If it is him, then perhaps the Fates
are not as cruel as I thought.

PRIEST
I'd like to know—
if I may be so bold—
what has brought you here like this?

DOROTEA
I owe you this much, gentlemen.
You must have heard,
for it was the talk of the town,
the unfortunate story,
that unhappy tale,
of the Marqués and Dorotea,
of Lucinda and Cardenio.

PRIEST　　　　We've just heard a little about that,
　　　　　　　from a credible witness—

CARDENIO　　Who said that Lucinda is as fickle
　　　　　　　as the wind and the water.

DOROTEA　　I believed that too, 2690
　　　　　　　but soon enough we all found out
　　　　　　　she is in fact the most constant woman
　　　　　　　these lands have ever seen.
　　　　　　　The Duke has a country house
　　　　　　　with beautiful gardens
　　　　　　　where he retires from time to time.
　　　　　　　Lucinda has found refuge there.
　　　　　　　Lisardo, Cardenio's father
　　　　　　　and servant to the Duke,
　　　　　　　looks after her in his stead. 2700
　　　　　　　There I learned
　　　　　　　that on the night of her wedding,
　　　　　　　as she gave the Marqués her hand
　　　　　　　and repeated her vows,
　　　　　　　Lucinda fell to the ground in a dead faint.
　　　　　　　In her sleeve they found a dagger,
　　　　　　　and in her breast a letter.

CARDENIO　　What are you saying?

DOROTEA　　(*Aside*) This must be Cardenio,
　　　　　　　I am certain of it now. 2710
　　　　　　　(*Aloud*) The letter, written in her own hand,
　　　　　　　declared that Cardenio is her true husband
　　　　　　　and the Marqués could never be.
　　　　　　　Then I spoke to her myself
　　　　　　　and she told me her intent
　　　　　　　had been to kill herself,
　　　　　　　but she could not,

             for shock and fear overcame her.
             In tears, she begged me
             to find Cardenio for her.   2720
             I wandered these mountains endlessly
             and lost my way among the hills,
             calling out for him,
             but only my echo answered.
             I could recognize him by his voice,
             though I wouldn't know his face
             for I only spoke to him once, in the dark.
             I search for him high and low,
             in the hopes that finding a path to him
             will lead to my own good fortune.   2730
             For I am Dorotea,
             the most wretched woman that ever lived,
             betrayed by the Marqués,
             a most unfortunate—

CARDENIO   My God, I am Cardenio!
             My lady, give me your hands.

DOROTEA   First you must read this letter,
             which refutes the accusations
             you've lodged against Lucinda.
             This is the letter they found in her breast.   2740
             I bring it straight from her hands to your eyes.

DOROTEA gives him the letter and CARDENIO reads it

BARBER   This is certainly very peculiar.

PRIEST   Remarkable, to be sure.

DOROTEA   Could this be how heaven
             intends to help me?

SANCHO   A letter! I'll be damned!
             Let me mind my own business.

CARDENIO   I'd know this beloved handwriting anywhere!
             These words undo the sting
             of an imagined betrayal.   2750
             Now if Lucinda cannot be mine,
             I'll at least die happy
             knowing that it was no fault of hers,
             but rather the will of heaven.
             Dorotea, may God keep you.
             I owe you so much,
             and though I am but a poor man
             I will forever seek to repay that debt.

DOROTEA   That's enough of that.
             Come with me.   2760

CARDENIO   Let's go, then.

PRIEST   Could we first assist
             this poor errant knight,
             if it's not too much trouble?

CARDENIO   Yes, of course.
             You helped bring about
             this happy resolution for me.

DOROTEA   It's only right we should assist you.

PRIEST   Follow me.

BARBER   How will we do it?   2770

PRIEST   I'll tell you on the way.
             Sancho, listen.

SANCHO	Oh I've been listening, but what if we find more hocus-pocus?
DOROTEA	I'm coming for you, Marqués!
CARDENIO	I'm coming to you, Lucinda!

Exit all

SCENE 4

A clearing in the mountains

Enter DON QUIXOTE

DON QUIXOTE Green fields, clear fountains,
 withered now by my fierce gaze.
 Ancient mountains, cavernous depths,
 look upon this my wild face. 2780
 Alas! I do but sigh,
 and yet you shrink from my voice.
 What a fortunate Spaniard I would be
 if my lady Dulcinea
 could take the place of the sun
 and watch me from above.
 Never shall another knight
 attempt such feats of madness.
 How could Sancho ever recount
 the things he saw me accomplish? 2790
 Frenzy and fury to surpass Orlando,
 and the first madman himself.
 Now calmly, softly, bit by bit,
 I'll display a madness most clever.
 I'll be a poet—clever and mad all at once.
 Measure by measure,

I'll count out the lines,
arranging their feet
as I arrange mine. (*Dances*)
A poet's brain is in their toes,   2800
so head over heels I go.
Shall I expand upon that thought?
No, lengthy footnotes are a bore.
How 'bout an ode to chivalric lore?
No, it's a tribute that can't be bought.
How 'bout a lovely, flowing sonnet?
Not enough rhymes here in my bonnet.
Yet rhyming couplets, no doubt,
are the best when love's about.
Mighty muses come to me!   2810
Oh! Is it Sancho that I see?
My stars, it is my squire.
To speak to him is my desire.
My friends, here is where I take a bow.
That's poetry enough for now.
Panza?

Enter SANCHO

SANCHO   Sir, hurry up
and put some clothes on.

DON QUIXOTE   What's the rush?

SANCHO   A princess is coming to see you.   2820
You need to look decent,
if not downright classy.
She is on her way.

DON QUIXOTE   Wait, hold on.
What did Dulcinea say?

SANCHO	Come on! Can't you see that lady there dismounting from her steed?

Enter CARDENIO, the PRIEST, the BARBER and DOROTEA unseen by DON QUIXOTE

PRIEST	(*To DOROTEA*) Now you'll be the damsel in distress.	
DOROTEA	The distress I can do, but I don't know about playing a damsel.	2830
BARBER	Don't be embarrassed.	
DOROTEA	Don't worry, I've studied my part.	
BARBER	Should we approach him now?	
PRIEST	Yes, let's.	

DOROTEA reveals herself to DON QUIXOTE while the rest stay hidden

DOROTEA	I kneel to you, my lord.	
DON QUIXOTE	Arise, beautiful maiden.	
DOROTEA	Oh brave knight! I shall not rise until you grant me a boon.	2840
DON QUIXOTE	I shall grant it, as long as it doesn't go against God, the king, or the oaths I swore to uphold as a knight.	

DOROTEA   Give me your invincible hands.

DON QUIXOTE Arise. Tell me who you are.

DOROTEA   I am the unfortunate
            Princess Micomicona,
            of the kingdom of Micomicón,   2850
            crossed and dispossessed.
            The giant Gatarau,
            he of the dreadful voice
            and the cross-eyed gaze,
            robbed me of all my hopes.
            He was in love with me
            and locked my father away
            because I refused to marry him.
            No man dares to fight him
            as he is a fearless brute.   2860
            Fatherless and in distress,
            I have come to faraway lands
            in search of you,
            spurred by tales of your courage.
            The whole world calls you the strong,
            the brave, the righter of wrongs,
            the one who gilded our tarnished age.
            You've accomplished so much,
            the very sight of your sword
            strikes fear into the hearts of men,   2870
            not to speak of your mighty arm.
            Pity me, who in my kingdom
            dined round the clock,
            and now wander from inn to inn,
            growing thinner by the second.
            I shed tears of blood,
            and long to—

DON QUIXOTE Say no more.

| | Rise, Your Highness.
I am your knight from this moment on
and I will settle this.
Oh monstruous giant, malformed creature,
look out, here I come!
Sancho, take my weapons down from that tree. | 2880 |

DOROTEA   I'll help you get ready.
             (*Aside*) God, keep me from laughing.

PRIEST   (*Aside*) Wasn't that incredible?

CARDENIO   (*Aside*) You're right,
             Dorotea did a great job.

BARBER   (*Aside*) She spoke so well.   2890

DON QUIXOTE Oh my weapons, your rest is over.
             We are together once again
             and ready for a great adventure.

DOROTEA   Let me help you gird your loins.

DON QUIXOTE That will certainly raise my spirits!

SANCHO   You look fierce!

PRIEST   (*To CARDENIO and BARBER*) Let's pretend to run
             into them.

DON QUIXOTE I'm on my way to reclaim Micomicón
             from your enemy, no matter his size.
             I swear this upon the sun,   2900
             even if more giants rain down from the sky
             than there are stars or atoms within them.
             Come along, noble princess.

DOROTEA May God grant you a thousand years.

Exit all

SCENE 5

A room in DUKE'*s palace*

Enter LISARDO *and* LUCINDA

LISARDO My lady, forgive me
if we can't serve you as you deserve.
This house isn't the same
since my wife fell ill.

LUCINDA Do not worry about my comfort.
Indeed, I only wish to serve you.   2910
I am truly sorry to hear about your wife.

LISARDO She has almost finished her will,
and then she will receive her last rites.

LUCINDA Take courage.

LISARDO Oh, how can I bear it?
How could I not weep
for my wife of thirty years?

LUCINDA Just think of it as Heaven's will.

LISARDO It's good to have women around,
from the beginning to the end of life.   2920

LUCINDA I would just like to see your son again,
if it's the last thing I do.

LISARDO	Cardenio's absence also adds to my grief, since this is a serious matter. If he takes much longer, he will lose you.
LUCINDA	His love for me will guide the way. Will you put on mourning clothes now?
LISARDO	Why should I? Clothes don't make the man. A shepherd's cloak and straw hat are my only mantle and crown. Long ago, my lord the Duke asked me to become a courtier, but I knew my place. But never mind that. The Marqués, mad with jealousy, is on his way here, determined to take you away. Mark my words, you will never be my daughter.
LUCINDA	If God gave me free will, how can any human betrayal ever take it away? I have everything I need to end my life: love, honor, my heart in my breast, and two hands.
LISARDO	But the Marqués is planning to take you from here today. He told me so himself.
LUCINDA	Is the Duke awake yet? I want to speak to him.
LISARDO	I'll go see.

Exit LISARDO. The MARQUÉS enters through one door with FULGENCIO and some SERVANTS behind him with masks on, while CARDENIO, DOROTEA, DON QUIXOTE, SANCHO, the PRIEST and the BARBER enter through another door

MARQUÉS	Bring her to me at once.
SERVANTS	We will, my lord.
CARDENIO	The Duke is my only hope! 2950
MARQUÉS	What perfect timing.
CARDENIO	Where did all these people come from?
LUCINDA	Oh no!
MARQUÉS	Not so fast.
CARDENIO	Wait!
LUCINDA	We are betrayed, my love!
CARDENIO	Your loyal servant will protect you from traitors and villains!
MARQUÉS	How dare you speak such words and raise your hands against me? 2960

DON QUIXOTE comes forward

DON QUIXOTE	Tis I who shall fight you!
MARQUÉS	Get this madman out of here!
BARBER	Help me, Sancho.

The BARBER grabs DON QUIXOTE and SANCHO tries to defend him

DON QUIXOTE	Let me go!

PRIEST	The Marqués will ruin our plan.

The PRIEST and BARBER restrain SANCHO and DON QUIXOTE,
pulling them both offstage

CARDENIO	Forgive him, he doesn't know who you are. My sword awaits you, my lord.	
MARQUÉS	I will sheath mine in your despicable breast!	
LUCINDA	No!	
DOROTEA	Marqués, my lord!	2970

LUCINDA attempts to intervene

LUCINDA	(*To CARDENIO*) I'll die to protect you.
MARQUÉS	(*To SERVANTS*) Kill him!

Enter the DUKE and more SERVANTS. The MARQUÉS and DUKE fight

DUKE	Cease this at once, oh treacherous son. Where are you going, you villain? Stop! I will spill your blood myself.	
MARQUÉS	No one will stop me this time!	
CARDENIO	The time for courtesy is over. My breast, if not my hand, must protect the Duke.	
DUKE	(*To MARQUÉS*) You're the devil himself! I must put an end to the man who treats us so vilely.	2980

DOROTEA attempts to intervene

DOROTEA   No! Though he may kill me with his scorn,
I can't bear to see him dead!

MARQUÉS   (*To his* SERVANTS) Kill the Duke!

FULGENCIO   Never! We are not traitors.
He's our former master,
and the only reason we obey you.

DUKE   Disarm him at once.
Give his weapons to the servants.

MARQUÉS   These are the wages of my sin.   2990

DUKE   I will have no more to do with him.
I will kill him myself,
or beg the King to lock him up
in a castle somewhere.
But wait, what are those cries I hear?

Enter LISARDO

LISARDO   Alas! My wife has just died.
Yet with her death,
Heaven has removed the cause
of your long affliction, my lord.
My prudent wife, a good Christian at the end,   3000
on her deathbed declared to a notary
and before multiple witnesses
that Cardenio is in fact Don Fernando,
the true Marqués and heir to your estate.
The man you know as the Marqués
is not Fernando, but Cardenio,
our son born in our humble bed.
And I, complicit in this ruse,
must pay for this with my life,

	though I might not have much left	3010
	after the loss of my wife.	
DUKE	What you now confirm I knew deep within.	
	The soul of an honest man	
	rarely, if ever, lies to him.	
	(*To* CARDENIO) Let me embrace you, my son.	
CARDENIO	Is this a dream?	
MARQUÉS	How has it come to this?	
CARDENIO	(*To* DUKE) Let me kiss your hand.	
DUKE	(*To* CARDENIO) Arise.	
DOROTEA	(*Aside*) Since fate has returned	3020
	everyone to their true station,	
	will my love return to me?	
LUCINDA	(*Aside*) Since Cardenio has undergone	
	this strange transformation,	
	will my love now abandon me?	
DUKE	(*To* CARDENIO) What troubles you?	
CARDENIO	One question consumes me.	
DUKE	I know what it must be	
	and it is time we resolve it.	
	Give your hand to Lucinda.	3030
CARDENIO	With my life and my soul.	
DUKE	This is how you nobly reward	
	the one who loved you as a peasant.	

CARDENIO	(*To* MARQUÉS) Give your hand to Dorotea.
MARQUÉS	I will.
DOROTEA	Though it is a humble hand now, I still treasure it.
DUKE	(*To* MARQUÉS) I only forgive your misdeeds for her sake.
FULGENCIO	Since this has all come to a happy end, let's go see how the Barber and the Priest 3040 finally get the madman home.

Enter DON QUIXOTE *inside a cage,*[32] *with the* PRIEST *and the* BARBER

DON QUIXOTE	Who trapped me in here? Was it the sorcerer Fristón-Arcalaus-Urganda?[33] Where are my sword and shield?
BARBER	Don't fret about being spellbound, Knight of the Sorrowful Countenance. This adventure will end at the very moment the Great Lion of La Mancha and the Dove of El Toboso, despite the doggedness of the Great Khan,[34] 3050 lie down in their wedding bed and bring forth puppies, as shining as the celestial Dogstar. So take heart! It's only a matter of time.

---

   32   The original staging would have involved a cage on pulleys, using more elaborate stage machinery than was common at the time of the play's writing.

   33   *Fristón-Arcalaus-Urganda*: A collection of good and bad sorcerers from the chivalric tradition and from Cervantes's novel.

   34   *Great Khan*: Orientalist references to an exoticized East are common in Spanish chivalric romances.

DON QUIXOTE Oh, divine prophecy!
            I'm so happy to hear it!
            This enchantment is bound to
            put me in the history books.

CARDENIO   And here ends the *comedia*
            of the sons switched at birth   3060
            and the errant knight
            Don Quixote de la Mancha.

Exit all

End of the Comedia of Don Quixote de la Mancha

www.ingramcontent.com/pod-product-compliance
Lightning Source LLC
Chambersburg PA
CBHW022105160426
43198CB00008B/360